SELECT SERMONS OF JOHN HENI

GEORGE CARTER

Published 2017

INTRODUCTION

Towards the middle of the 19th century, a scant half a dozen or so years after Victoria ascended the throne of Imperial England, so-called "polite society" in that country was shocked to read in the Times of London, the "newspaper of record," that John Henry Newman had abandoned both the powerful and dominating English state and the established Anglican Church to embrace the Roman Catholic Church. Why would this erudite and highly thought of English churchman leave the religion of his forefathers and become an underling of that man in Rome who English "impolite society" referred to as "Old Red Socks" or "The Whore of Babylon"? This book attempts to answer that question by bringing to the public Newman's spiritual thinking on his road to and in Rome in sixteen of his Anglican and Catholic sermons.

CONTENTS

After each sermon space is provided for a reflection.

A.   ANGLICAN
8

RELIGIOUS PILGRIMAGE

John Henry Newman, Cong. Orat., (February 21, 1801–11 August 11, 1890), a Catholic cardinal and theologian, was an important figure in the religious history of England in the 19th century. He was known nationally by the mid-1830s. Originally an evangelical Oxford University academic and priest in the Church of England, Newman then became drawn to the High Church tradition of Anglicanism.

He became known as a leader of, and an able polemicist for, the Oxford Movement, an influential and controversial grouping of Anglicans who wished to return to the Church of England many Catholic beliefs and liturgical rituals from before the English Reformation. In this the movement had some success. However, in 1845 Newman, joined by some but not all of his followers, left the Church of England and his teaching post at Oxford University and was received into the Catholic Church. He was quickly ordained as a priest and continued as an influential religious leader and preacher, based in Birmingham at the oratory he set up in that city.

In 1879, he was created a cardinal by Pope Leo XIII in recognition of his services to the cause of the Catholic Church in England. He was instrumental in the founding of the Catholic University of Ireland, which evolved into University College, Dublin, today the largest university in Ireland.

Newman's beatification was officially proclaimed by Pope Benedict on September19 2010 during his visit to the United Kingdom.

Newman was also a literary figure of note: his major writings include "The Tracts of the Times" (1833–1841), his autobiography "Apologia Pro Vita Sua" (1865–66), "The Grammar of Assent" (1870), and the poem "The Dream of Gerontius" (1865), which was set to music in 1900 by Edgar Elgar.

CONVERSION.

On 25 September 1843, the Reverend John Henry Newman, Vicar of one of the most famous churches in England, St Mary's Oxford, preached his last sermon as an Anglican at Littlemore, (a satellite parish of St Mary's where he now lived in a small community of men living in an interesting "monastic" experiment in Anglican Catholicism.) He asked the congregation to, "pray for him, that in all things he may know God's will, and at all times he may be ready to fulfill it." He was still two years away from his reception into what he was to call "The One True Fold", and which in England at that time was still generally referred to as "Roman" Catholicism.

It is not necessary to over-complicate Newman's conversion, despite it taking him the better part of seven years to make the final step. Nor indeed do we need to over-complicate (or over-liberalize) his Catholicism. His conversion was, as his last Anglican sermon puts it, Newman simply doing God's will, and his Catholicism, simply his fulfillment of God's will. It took Newman seven years to finally determine God's will for his future — for many of us a lifetime is not enough.

Newman wanted certitude that what he was doing was not the result of his own private judgment, but was God's will. He was surrounded by a world, political and scientific, that was increasingly positioning private judgment over God's truths. A world we can see which today has taken that judgment to ludicrous extremes, which worships the individual, and turns its back on God. But this certitude for Newman — a highly skilled mathematician — would not come from his logical reasoning about Church history and development — it could, for Newman, only come from God — and it led him to the Catholic Church.

He was not like so many Catholic converts, now and then, introduced to the Catholic Church by a friend; he had little or no interest in the rituals, *per se*, of Catholicism, in fact knew nothing of them in any real detail until after his reception; he was not at all interested in what we might call the "vestments and vestures" drama of Catholicism as many were; nor indeed, in Gothic revivalism, which brought so many into the Church at that time. Newman's conversion resulted from engagement with, and acceptance of, what he considered to be undeniable and non-negotiable, absolute, *objective*, revealed truths about the supernatural *not* the natural world.

Put simply, his interest lay in being sure that the O*ne True* Church would be the Church where he could have the certitude of knowing that within that Church, *he could save his soul*.

Simple as that? Surely not? After all, we are talking about one of the leading intellects of his day; a serious and significant scholar; a major theologian and Oxford Don — the leader of a major movement to reinject Catholicism back into the Anglican Church; the writer of numerous books and tracts and famous to the point that rarely a day would go by without something in the newspapers about him. Surely, his conversion has to be more complicated that this? At its very heart, no! Salvation is the key to understanding Newman's conversion because he had come to the certain belief that the Anglican Church was in schism, and so therefore unable to be the vehicle of Christ's salvific grace. "The simple question is", he wrote, "Can I (it is personal, not whether another, but can I) be saved in the English Church? Am I in safety, were I to die tonight?" What would a non-Catholic reader's answer to that question be?

Newman's was clear. He believed he was not in safety where he was, and so turned his back on the establishment Church in England; a well-paid job; an Oxford Fellowship; status and standing; family and friends. This was no lifestyle choice; no modern day sea change or "tree-change"; no "new age seeking" after material well-being. This was supernatural conversion —not to the accidents of Catholic ritual to suit life here on earth— but to the substance of what Newman was to call the "awful reality" of the Catholic Church.

What Newman did in becoming a Catholic in a mid-19th Century world where the privileging of *man* and the natural world was taking over in all spheres of activity and thinking (as it is doing so even more today); where unbelief was growing exponentially; where science and engineering were the new gods. What Newman did made him stand out from the world of Imperial privilege and status. He stood out *not* because he became a Catholic as such — but because he stood out *for the salvation of his soul* over and above everything else in the world of Anglican religious indifference and the unbelief that surrounded him. His becoming a Catholic to save his soul (and not because he liked the "bells and smells") was a total indictment of, and embarrassment to, not only Erastian Anglicanism, but also to the State itself. It was a very public celebration of the religious over the secular.

He wrote, many years before his conversion that, "The Church of Christ... is not an institution of man, not a mere political establishment, not a creature of the state, depending on the state's breath, made and unmade at its will, but it is a Divine society, a great work of God". Sixteen years later, by the act of his conversion as a salvific move made possible *only* supernaturally, he revealed the unthinkable at this time of British Victorian supremacy of the world, that neither of the prime English institutions, the Anglican Church or the British Empire —both growing in influence and importance around the whole world — that neither of these bastions of 19th century Victorian security and prosperity, *was capable of saving a man's soul.*

In doing what he did, at the time he did it, Newman broke all the rules of a Victorian England, gloriously self-confident in its abilities to control the entire world. He ran up to the palace gates and shouted out loudly the truth about the Empresses' new clothes. This is not the hypersensitive, timid, "souffre-douleur", as Newman is so often thought to have been. This is the act of a very brave man — brave not because of his own Victorian self-assuredness — but because of his certitude that Catholicism, and not England and its Church, knew how to save his soul.

At a time when Empire was becoming the be-all and end-all of what it meant to be British; when buildings —whole towns and cities — were being built on such a scale and solidity to scream out to everyone who saw them, "this building and all it stands for politically, socially, culturally and economically will last 1,000 years," (shades of the later Third Reich?) Newman stuck a pin into the balloon and blew apart the myth, in a way no one had really done before him, that the State and its Church, were simply a chimera and could never offer real and lasting salvation to their people, despite all the appearances and their tub-thumping, that they could.

And he did this — privileging the supernatural over the natural — not by writing a book about it, though reflections emerged later; not by preaching sermons at the time, although his sermons both before and after 1845 do offer clues about his spiritual thinking; but by a simple action, taken thoughtfully and carefully, of actually becoming a Catholic. He did this, in the end, quickly and without fanfare. He didn't seek instruction; he didn't call on his high status contacts like the then Bishop Wiseman to receive him with pomp and ceremony in glorious Gothic splendor, or map out a career path for himself as Anglican Archdeacon, later Cardinal, Manning was to do immediately after his own conversion. He was received by (the now Blessed) Fr. Dominic Barberi, following a cold, wet and windy night at Littlemore, on 9 October 1845 in a converted farm shed for a chapel. A shed, which in its rude structure, one might compare to the stable in Bethlehem.

A month later he wrote in a letter, "Pray be quite assured that I would not have left the English church had I thought it possible for me to remain in God's favor and remain a member of it. To my own mind it is as clear as light that it is a church, which the Fathers would not have acknowledged. I had no alternative but to leave it unless I gave up the Fathers, nay all revealed religion." This is totally uncompromising. And we do Newman a very grave disservice, and indeed the enormous power of the supernatural action involved in his conversion, if we temper such uncompromising statements (as many now do) to make them suit more ecumenical times. Times that often include an attempted watering down of Catholic doctrine.

The rite of reception in the *Rituale Romanum* asks of the convert, and Fr. Dominic would have asked this of Newman, *"Quid petis ab Ecclesia?"* (What do you seek from the Church?), and Newman would have answered, *"Fides"* (Faith). And then Fr. Dominic from that same *Rituale* would have asked, *"Fides quid tibi praestet?"* (What might that faith offer you?). Two little words — that's all — was Newman's answer — *"Vitam Aeternam"* (Eternal Life). Nothing more. Nothing less.

So, let the reader peruse these sixteen sermons, given between 1825 and 1873. If they are of a mind, at the end of each one in the space provided they might for their own edification write a reflection on it.

SERMONS

A. ANGLICAN.

I. Temporal Advantages. January 23, 1825
"We brought nothing into this world, and it is certain we can carry nothing out. And having food and raiment let us be therewith content."—1 Tim. vi. 7, 8.

Every age has its own special sins and temptations. Impatience with their lot, murmuring, grudging, unthankfulness, discontent, are sins common to men at all times, but I suppose one of those sins which belongs to our age more than to another, is desire of a greater portion of worldly goods than God has given us, —ambition and covetousness in one shape or another. This is an age and country in which, more than in any other, men have the opportunity of what is called rising in life, —of changing from a lower to a higher class of society, of gaining wealth; and upon wealth all things follow, —consideration, credit, influence, power, enjoyment, the lust of the flesh, and the lust of the eyes, and the pride of life. Since, then, men now-a-days have so often the opportunity of gaining worldly goods which formerly they had not, it is not wonderful they should be tempted to gain them; nor wonderful that when they have gained them, they should set their heart upon them.

And it will often happen, that from coveting them before they are gained, and from making much of them when they are gained, men will be led to take unlawful means, whether to increase them, or not to lose them. But I am not going so far as to suppose the case of dishonesty, fraud, double-dealing, injustice, or the like: to these St. Paul seems to allude when he goes on to say, "They that will be rich fall into temptation and a snare;" again, "The love of money is the root of all evil."

But let us confine ourselves to the consideration of the nature itself, and the natural effects, of these worldly things, without extending our view to those further evils to which they may give occasion. St. Paul says in the text, that we ought to be content with food and raiment; and the wise man says, "Give me neither poverty nor riches; feed me with food convenient for me [1]." And our Lord would have us "take no thought for the morrow," which surely is a dissuasion from aggrandizing ourselves, accumulating wealth, or aiming at distinction. And He has taught us when we pray to say, "Give us this day our *daily* bread." Yet a great number of persons, I may say, nearly all men, are not content with enough, they are not satisfied with sufficiency; they wish for something more than simplicity, and plainness, and gravity, and modesty, in their mode of living; they like show and splendor, and admiration from the many, and obsequiousness on the part of those who have to do with them, and the ability to do as they will; they like to attract the eye, to be received with consideration and respect, to be heard with deference, to be obeyed with promptitude; they love greetings in the markets, and the highest seats; they like to be well dressed, and to have titles of honor. Now, then, I will attempt to show that these gifts of the world which men seek are not to be reckoned good things; that they are ill suited to our nature and our present state, and are dangerous to us; that it is on the whole best for our prospects of happiness even here, not to say hereafter, that we should be without them.

Now, first, that these worldly advantages, as they are called, are not productive of any great enjoyment even now to the persons possessing them, it does not require many words to prove. I might indeed maintain, with no slight show of reason, that these things, so far from increasing happiness, are generally the source of much disquietude; that as a person has more wealth, or more power, or more distinction, his cares generally increase, and his time is less his own: thus, in the words of the preacher, "the abundance of the rich will not suffer him to sleep," and, "in much wisdom is much grief, and he that increaseth knowledge increaseth sorrow [2]." But however this may be, at least these outward advantages do not increase our happiness. Let me ask any one who has succeeded in any object of his desire, has he experienced in his success that full, that lasting satisfaction which he anticipated? Did not some feeling of disappointment, of weariness, of satiety, of disquietude, after a short time, steal over his mind? I think it did; and if so; what reason has he to suppose that that greater share of reputation, opulence, and influence which he has not, and which he desires, would, if granted him, suffice to make him happy? No; the fact is certain, however slow and unwilling we may be to believe it, none of these things bring the pleasure, which we beforehand suppose they will bring. Watch narrowly the persons who possess them, and you will at length discover the same uneasiness and occasional restlessness which others have; you will find that there is just a something beyond, which they are striving after, or just some one thing which annoys and distresses them. The good things you admire please for the most part only while they are new; now those who have them are accustomed to them, so they care little for them, and find no alleviation in them of the anxieties and cares which still remain. It is fine, in prospect and imagination, to be looked up to, admired, applauded, courted, feared, to have a name among men, to rule their opinions or their actions by our word, to create a stir by our movements, while men cry, "Bow the knee," before us; but none knows so well how vain is the world's praise, as he who has it. And why is this?

It is, in a word, because the soul was made for religious employments and pleasures; and hence, that no temporal blessings, however exalted or refined, can satisfy it. As well might we attempt to sustain the body on chaff, as to feed and nourish the immortal soul with the pleasures and occupations of the world.

Only thus much, then, shall I say on the point of worldly advantages not bringing present happiness. But next, let us consider that, on the other hand, they are positively dangerous to our eternal interests.

Many of these things, if they did no other harm, at least are injurious to our souls, by taking up the time that might else be given to religion. Much intercourse with the world, which eminence and station render a duty, has a tendency to draw off the mind from God, and deaden it to the force of religious motives and considerations. There is a want of sympathy between much business and calm devotion, great splendor and a simple faith, which will be to no one more painful than to the Christian, to whom God has assigned some post of especial responsibility or distinction. To maintain a religious spirit in the midst of engagements and excitements of this world is possible only to a saint; nay, the case is the same though our business be one of a charitable and religious nature, and though our chief intercourse is with those whom we believe to have their minds set upon religion, and whose principles and conduct are not likely to withdraw our feet from the narrow way of life. For here we are likely to be deceived from the very circumstance that our employments are religious; and our end, as being a right one, will engross us, and continually tempt us to be inattentive to the means, and to the spirit in which we pursue it.

Our Lord alludes to the danger of multiplied occupations in the Parable of the Sower: "He that received seed among thorns, is he that heareth the word, and the cares of this world and the deceitfulness of riches choke the word, and he becometh unfruitful."

Again, these worldly advantages, as they are called, will seduce us into an excessive love of them. We are too well inclined by nature to live by sight, rather than by faith; and besides the immediate enjoyment, there is something so agreeable to our natural tastes in the honors and emoluments of the world, that it requires an especially strong mind, and a large measure of grace, not to be gradually corrupted by them. We are led to set our hearts upon them, and in the same degree to withdraw them from God. We become unwilling to leave this visible state of things, and to be reduced to a level with those multitudes who are at present inferior to ourselves. Prosperity is sufficient to seduce, although not to satisfy. Hence death and judgment are unwelcome subjects of reflection to the rich and powerful; for death takes from them those comforts which habit has made necessary to them, and throws them adrift on a new order of things, of which they know nothing, save that in it there is no respect of persons.

And as these goods lead us to love the world, so again do they lead us to trust in the world: we not only become worldly-minded, but unbelieving; our wills becoming corrupt, our understandings also become dark, and disliking the truth, we gradually learn to maintain and defend error. St. Paul speaks of those who "having put away a good conscience, concerning faith made shipwreck [3]." Familiarity with this world makes men discontented with the doctrine of the narrow way; they fall into heresies, and attempt to attain salvation on easier terms than those which Christ holds out to us. In a variety of ways this love of the world operates. Men's opinions are imperceptibly formed by their wishes. If, for instance, we see our worldly prospects depend, humanly speaking, upon a certain person, we are led to court him, to honor him, and adopt his views, and trust in an arm of flesh, till we forget the overruling power of God's providence, and the necessity of His blessing, for the building of the house and the keeping of the city.

And moreover, these temporal advantages, as they are considered, have a strong tendency to render us self-confident. When a man has been advanced in the world by means of his own industry and skill, when he began poor and ends rich, how apt will he be to pride himself, and confide, in his own contrivances and his own resources! Or when a man feels himself possessed of good abilities; of quickness in entering into a subject, or of powers of argument to discourse readily upon it, or of acuteness to detect fallacies in dispute with little effort, or of a delicate and cultivated taste, so as to separate with precision the correct and beautiful in thought and feeling from the faulty and irregular, how will such an one be tempted to self-complacency and self-approbation! How apt will he be to rely upon himself, to rest contented with himself, to be harsh and impetuous; or supercilious; or to be fastidious, indolent, unpractical; and to despise the pure, self-denying, humble temper of religion, as something irrational, dull, enthusiastic, or needlessly rigorous!

These considerations on the extreme danger of possessing temporal advantages will be greatly strengthened by considering the conduct of holy men when gifted with them. Take, for instance, Hezekiah, one of the best of the Jewish kings. He, too, had been schooled by occurrences, which one might have thought would have beaten down all pride and self-esteem. The king of Assyria had come against him, and seemed prepared to overwhelm him with his hosts;

and he had found his God a mighty Deliverer, cutting off in one night of the enemy an hundred fourscore and five thousand men. And again, he had been miraculously recovered from sickness, when the sun's shadow turned ten degrees back, to convince him of the certainty of the promised recovery. Yet when the king of Babylon sent ambassadors to congratulate him on this recovery, we find this holy man ostentatiously displaying to them his silver, and gold, and armor. Truly the heart is "deceitful above all things;" and it was, indeed, to manifest this more fully that God permitted him thus to act. God "left him," says the inspired writer, "to try him, that he might know all that was in his heart [4]."

Let us take David as another instance of the great danger of prosperity; he, too, will exemplify the unsatisfactory nature of temporal goods; for which, think you, was the happier, the lowly shepherd or the king of Israel? Observe his simple reliance on God and his composure, when advancing against Goliath: "The Lord," he says, "that delivered me out of the paw of the lion and out of the paw of the bear, He will deliver me out of the hand of this Philistine [5]." And compare this with his grievous sins, his continual errors, his weaknesses, inconsistencies, and then his troubles and mortifications after coming to the throne of Israel; and who will not say that his advancement was the occasion of both sorrow and sin, which, humanly speaking, he would have escaped, had he died amid the sheepfolds of Jesse? He was indeed most wonderfully sustained by Divine grace, and died in the fear of God; yet what right-minded and consistent Christian but must shrink from the bare notion of possessing a worldly greatness so corrupting and seducing as David's kingly power was shown to be in the instance of so great a Saint?

The case of Solomon is still more striking; his falling away even surpasses our anticipation of what our Savior calls "the deceitfulness of riches." He may indeed, for what we know, have repented; but at least the history tells us nothing of it. All we are told is, that "King Solomon loved many strange women . . . and it came to pass when Solomon was old, that his wives turned away his heart after other gods; and his heart was not perfect with the Lord his God, as was the heart of David his father. For Solomon went after Ashtaroth, the goddess of the Sidonians, and after Milcom, the abomination of the Ammonites [6]." Yet this was he who had offered up that most sublime and affecting prayer at the Dedication of the Temple, and who, on a former occasion, when the Almighty gave him the choice of any blessing he should ask, had preferred an understanding heart to long life, and honor, and riches.

So dangerous, indeed, is the possession of the goods of this world, that, to judge from the Scripture history, seldom has God given unmixed prosperity to any one whom He loves. "Blessed is the man," says the Psalmist, "whom Thou chastenest, and teachest him out of Thy law [7]." Even the best men require some pain or grief to sober them and keep their hearts right. Thus, to take the example of St. Paul himself, even his labors, sufferings, and anxieties, he tells us, would not have been sufficient to keep him from being exalted above measure, through the abundance of the revelations, unless there had been added some further cross, some "thorn in the flesh [8]," as he terms it, some secret affliction, of which we are not particularly informed, to humble him, and to keep him in a sense of his weak and dependent condition.

The history of the Church after him affords us an additional lesson of the same serious truth. For three centuries it was exposed to heathen persecution; during that long period God's Hand was upon His people: what did they do when that Hand was taken off? How did they act when the world was thrown open to them, and the saints possessed the high places of the earth? Did they enjoy it? far from it, they shrank from that which they might, had they chosen, have made much of; they denied themselves what was set before them; when God's Hand was removed, their own hand was heavy upon them. Wealth, honor, and power, they put away from them. They recollected our Lord's words, "How hardly shall they that have riches enter into the kingdom of God [9]!" And St. James's, "Hath not God chosen the poor of this world, rich in faith, and heirs of the kingdom [10]?" For three centuries they had no need to think of those words, for Christ remembered them, and kept them humble; but when He left them to themselves, then they did voluntarily what they had hitherto suffered patiently. They were resolved that the Gospel character of a Christian should be theirs. Still, as before, Christ spoke of His followers as poor and weak, and lowly and simple-minded; men of plain lives, men of prayer, not "faring sumptuously," or clad in "soft raiment," or "taking thought for the morrow." They recollected what He said to the young Ruler, "If thou wilt be perfect, go and sell that thou hast, and give to the poor, and thou shalt have treasure in heaven, and come and follow Me." And so they put off their "gay clothing," their "gold, and pearls, and costly array;" they "sold that they had, and gave alms;" they "washed one another's feet;" they "had all things common." They formed themselves into communities for prayer and praise, for labor and study, for the care of the poor, for mutual edification, and preparation for Christ; and thus, as soon as the world professed to be Christian, Christians at once set up among them a witness against the world, and kings and monks came into the Church together. And from that time to this, never has the union of the Church with the State prospered, but when the Church was in union also with the hermitage and the cell.

Moreover, in those religious ages, Christians avoided greatness in the Church as well as in the world. They would not accept rank and station on account of their spiritual peril, when they were no longer encompassed by temporal trials.

When they were elected to the episcopate, when they were appointed to the priesthood, they fled away and hid themselves. They recollected our Lord's words, "Whosoever will be chief among you, let him be your servant;" and again, "Be not ye called Rabbi, for one is your Master, even Christ, and all ye are brethren [11]." And when discovered and forced to the eminence, which they shunned, they made much lament, and were in many tears. And they felt that their higher consideration in the world demanded of them some greater strictness and self-denial in their course of life, lest it should turn to a curse, lest the penance of which it would defraud them here, should be visited on them in manifold measure hereafter. They feared to have "their good things" and "their consolation" on earth, lest they should not have Lazarus' portion in heaven.

That state of things indeed is now long passed away, but let us not miss the doctrinal lesson, which it conveys, if we will not take it for our pattern. Before I conclude, however, I must take notice of an objection, which may be made to what I have been saying. It may be asked, "Are not these dangerous things the gifts of God? Are they not even called blessings? Did not God bestow riches and honor upon Solomon as a reward? And did He not praise him for praying for wisdom? And does not St. Paul say, 'Covet earnestly the best gifts [12]?'" It is true; nor did I ever mean to say that these things were bad in themselves, but bad, for us, if we seek them as ends, and dangerous to us from their fascination. "Every creature of God is good," as St. Paul says, "and nothing to be refused [13];" but circumstances may make good gifts injurious in our particular case. Wine is good in itself, but not for a man in a fever. If our souls were in perfect health, riches and authority, and strong powers of mind, would be very suitable to us: but they are weak and diseased, and require so great a grace of God to bear these advantages well, that we may be well content to be without them.

Still it may be urged, Are we then absolutely to give them up if we have them, and not accept them when offered? It may be a duty to keep them, it is sometimes a duty to accept them; for in certain cases God calls upon us not so much to put them away, as to put away our old natures, and make us new hearts and new spirits, wherewith to receive them. At the same time, it is merely for our safety to know their perilous nature, and to beware of them, and in no case to take them simply for their own sake, but with a view to God's glory. They must be instruments in our hands to promote the cause of Gospel truth. And, in this light, they have their value, and impart their real pleasure; but be it remembered, that value and that happiness are imparted by the end to which they are dedicated; It is "the altar that sanctifieth the gift [14]:" but, compared with the end to which they must be directed, their real and intrinsic excellence is little indeed.

In this point of view it is that we are to covet earnestly the best gifts: for it is a great privilege to be allowed to serve the Church. Have we wealth? Let it be the means of extending the knowledge of the truth—abilities? Of recommending it —power? Of defending it.

From what I have said concerning the danger of possessing the things which the world admires, we may draw the following rule: use them, as far as given, with gratitude for what is really good in them, and with a desire to promote God's glory by means of them, but do not go out of the way to seek them. They will not on the whole make you happier, and they may make you less religious.

For us, indeed, who are all the adopted children of God our Savior, what addition is wanting to complete our happiness? What can increase their peace who believe and trust in the Son of God? Shall we add a drop to the ocean, or grains to the sand of the sea? Shall we ask for an earthly inheritance, who have the fullness of an heavenly one; power, when in prayer we can use the power of Christ, or wisdom, guided as we may be by the true Wisdom and Light of men?

It is in this sense that the Gospel of Christ is a leveler of ranks: we pay, indeed, our superiors full reverence, and with cheerfulness as unto the Lord; and we honor eminent talents as deserving admiration and reward, and the more readily act we thus, because these are little things to pay. The time is short, year follows year, and the world is passing away. It is of small consequence to those who are beloved of God, and walk in the Spirit of truth, whether they pay or receive honor, which is but transitory and profitless. To the true Christian the world assumes another and more interesting appearance; it is no longer a stage for the great and noble, for the ambitious to fret in, and the wealthy to revel in; but it is a scene of probation. Every soul is a candidate for immortality. And the more we realize this view of things, the more will the accidental distinctions of nature or fortune die away from our view, and we shall be led habitually to pray, that upon every Christian may descend, in rich abundance, not merely worldly goods, but that heavenly grace which alone can turn this world to good account for us, and make it the path of peace and of life everlasting.

[1] Prov. xxx. 8.
[2] Eccles. i. 18.
[3] 1 Tim. i. 19.
[4] 2 Chron. xxxii. 31.
[5] 1 Sam. xvii. 37.
[6] 1 Kings xi. 1, 4, 5.
[7] Ps. xciv. 12.
[8] 2 Cor. xii. 7.
[9] Mark x. 23.
[10] James ii. 5.
[11] Matt. xx. 27, xxiii. 8

Reflection.

II. Religion Weariness to the Natural Man. July 27, 1828

"He hath no form nor comeliness; and when we shall see Him, there is no beauty that we should desire Him."—Isaiah liii. 2.

"Religion is a weariness;" such is the judgment commonly passed, often avowed, concerning the greatest of blessings which Almighty God has bestowed upon us. And when God gave the blessing, He at the same time foretold that such would be the judgment of the world upon it, even as manifested in the gracious Person of Him whom He sent to give it to us. "He hath no form nor comeliness," says the Prophet, speaking of our Lord and Savior, "and when we shall see Him, there is no beauty that we should desire Him." He declared beforehand, that to man His religion would be uninteresting and distasteful.

Not that this prediction excuses our deadness to it; this dislike of the religion given us by God Himself, seen as it is on all sides of us, —of religion in all its parts, whether its doctrines, its precepts, its polity, its worship, its social influence, —this distaste for its very name, must obviously be an insult to the Giver. But the text speaks of it as a fact, without commenting on the guilt involved in it; and as such I wish you to consider it, as far as this may be done in reverence and seriousness. Putting aside for an instant the thought of the ingratitude and the sin which indifference to Christianity implies, let us, as far as we dare, view it merely as a matter of fact, after the manner of the text, and form a judgment on the probable consequences of it. Let us take the state of the case as it is found, and survey it dispassionately, as even an unbeliever might survey it, without at the moment considering whether it is sinful or not; as a misfortune, if we will, or a strange accident, or a necessary condition of our nature, —one of the phenomena, as it may be called, of the present world. Let me then review human life in some of its stages and conditions, in order to impress upon you the fact of this contrariety between ourselves and our Maker: He having one will, we another; He declaring one thing to be good for us, and we fancying other objects to be our good.

1. "Religion is a weariness," alas! So feel even children before they can well express their meaning. Exceptions of course now and then occur; and of course children are always more open to religious impressions and visitations than grown persons. They have many good thoughts and good desires, of which, in after life, the multitude of men seem incapable. Yet who, after all, can have a doubt that, in spite of the more intimate presence of God's grace with those who have not yet learned to resist it, still, on the whole, religion is weariness to children? Consider their amusements, their enjoyments, —what they hope, what they devise, what they scheme, and what they dream about themselves in time future, when they grow up; and say what place religion holds in their

hearts. Watch the reluctance with which they turn to religious duties, to saying their prayers, or reading the Bible; and then judge.

Observe, as they get older, the influence which the fear of the ridicule of their companions has in deterring them even from speaking of religion, or seeming to be religious. Now the dread of ridicule, indeed, is natural enough; but why should religion inspire ridicule? What is there absurd in thinking of God? Why should we be ashamed of worshipping Him? It is unaccountable, but it is natural. We may call it an accident, or what we will; still it is an undeniable fact, and that is what I insist upon. I am not forgetful of the peculiar character of children's minds: sensible objects first meet their observation; it is not wonderful that they should at first be inclined to limit their thoughts to things of sense. A distinct profession of faith, and a conscious maintenance of principle, may imply a strength and consistency of thought to which they are as yet unequal. Again, childhood is capricious, ardent, and lighthearted; it cannot think deeply or long on any subject. Yet all this is not enough to account for the fact in question—why they should feel this distaste for the very subject of religion. Why should they be ashamed of paying reverence to an unseen, all-powerful God, whose existence they do not disbelieve? Yet they do feel ashamed of it. Is it that they are ashamed of themselves, not of their religion; feeling the inconsistency of professing what they cannot fully practice? This refinement does not materially alter the view of the case; for it is merely their own acknowledgment that they do not love religion as much as they ought. No; we seem compelled to the conclusion, that there is by nature some strange discordance between what we love and what God loves. So much, then, on the state of boyhood.

2. "Religion is a weariness." I will next take the case of young persons when they first enter into life. Here I may appeal to some perhaps who now hear me. Alas! My brethren, is it not so? Is not religion associated in your minds with gloom, melancholy, and weariness? I am not at present going so far as to reprove you for it, though I might well do so, if I did, perhaps you might at once turn away, and I wish you calmly to think the matter over, and bear me witness that I state the fact correctly. It is so; you cannot deny it. The very terms "religion," "devotion," "piety," "conscientiousness," "mortification," and the like, you find to be inexpressibly dull and cheerless: you cannot find fault with them, indeed, you would if you could; and whenever the words are explained in particulars and realized, then you do find occasion for exception and objection. But though you cannot deny the claims of religion used as a

vague and general term, yet how irksome, cold, uninteresting, uninviting, does it at best appear to you! How severe its voice! How forbidding its aspect!

With what animation, on the contrary, do you enter into the mere pursuits of time and the world! What bright anticipations of joy and happiness flit before your eyes! How you are struck and dazzled at the view of the prizes of this life, as they are called! How you admire the elegancies of art, the brilliance of wealth, or the force of intellect! According to your opportunities you mix in the world, you meet and converse with persons of various conditions and pursuits, and are engaged in the numberless occurrences of daily life. You are full of news; yon know what this or that person is doing, and what has befallen him; what has not happened, which was near happening, what may happen. You are full of ideas and feelings upon all that goes on around you. But, from some cause or other, religion has no part, no sensible influence, in your judgment of men and things. It is out of your way.

Perhaps you have your pleasure parties; you readily take your share in them time after time; you pass continuous hours in society where you know that it is quite impossible even to mention the name of religion. Your heart is in scenes and places when conversation on serious subjects is strictly forbidden by the rules of the world's propriety. I do not say we should discourse on religious subjects, wherever we go; I do not say we should make an effort to discourse on them at any time, nor that we are to refrain from social meetings in which religion does not lie on the surface of the conversation: but I do say, that when men find their pleasure and satisfaction to lie in society which proscribes religion, and when they deliberately and habitually prefer those amusements which have necessarily nothing to do with religion, such persons cannot view religion as God views it. And this is the point: that the feelings of our hearts on the subject of religion are different from the declared judgment of God; that we have a natural distaste for that which He has said is our chief good.

3. Now let us pass to the more active occupations of life. Here, too, religion is confessedly felt to be wearisome, it is out of place. The transactions of worldly business, speculations in trade, ambitious hopes, the pursuit of knowledge, the public occurrences of the day, these find a way directly to the heart, they rouse, they influence. It is superfluous to go about to prove this innate power over us of things of time and sense, to make us think and act. The name of religion, on the other hand, is weak and impotent; it contains no spell to kindle the feelings

of man, to make the heart beat with anxiety, and to produce activity and perseverance.

The reason is not merely that men are in want of leisure, and are sustained in a distressing continuance of exertion, by their duties towards those dependent on them. They have their seasons of relaxation, they turn for a time from their ordinary pursuits; still religion does not attract them, they find nothing of comfort or satisfaction in it. For a time they allow themselves to be idle. They want an object to employ their minds upon; they pace to and fro in very want of an object; yet their duties to God, their future hopes in another state of being, the revelation of God's mercy and will, as contained in Scripture, the news of redemption, the gift of regeneration, the sanctities, the devotional heights, the nobleness and perfection which Christ works in His elect, do not suggest themselves as fit subjects to dispel their weariness. Why? Because religion makes them melancholy, say they, and they wish to relax. Religion is a labor; it is weariness, a greater weariness than the doing nothing at all. "Wherefore," says Solomon, "is there a price in the hand of a fool to get wisdom, seeing he hath no heart to it [1]?"

4. But this natural contrariety between man and his Maker is still more strikingly shown by the confessions of men of the world who have given some thought to the subject, and have viewed society with somewhat of a philosophical spirit. Such men treat the demands of religion with disrespect and negligence, on the ground of their being unnatural. They say, "It is natural for men to love the world for its own sake; to be engrossed in its pursuits, and to set their hearts on the rewards of industry, on the comforts, luxuries, and pleasures of this life.

 Man would not be man if he could be made otherwise; he would not be what he was evidently intended for by his Maker." Let us pass by the obvious *answer* that might be given to this objection; it is enough for my purpose that it is *commonly urged*, recognizing as it does the fact of the disagreement existing between the claims of God's word, and the inclinations and natural capacities of man. Many, indeed, of those unhappy men who have denied the Christian faith, treat the religious principle altogether as a mere unnatural, eccentric state of mind, a peculiar untoward condition of the affections to which weakness will reduce a man, whether it has been brought on by anxiety, oppressive sorrow, bodily disease, excess of imagination or the like, and temporary or permanent, according to the circumstances of the disposing cause; a state to which we all are liable, as we are liable to any other mental injury, but unmanly and unworthy of our dignity as rational beings. Here again it is enough for our purpose, that it is allowed by these persons that the love of religion is unnatural and inconsistent with the original condition of our minds.

The same remark may be made upon the notions, which secretly prevail in certain quarters at the present day, concerning the unsuitableness of Christianity to an enlightened age. Men there are who look upon the inspired word of God with a sort of indulgence, as if it had its use, and had done service in its day; that in times of ignorance it awed and controlled fierce barbarians, whom nothing else could have subdued; but that from its very claim to be divine and infallible, and its consequent unalterableness, it is an obstacle to the improvement of the human race beyond a certain point, and must ultimately fall before the gradual advancement of mankind in knowledge and virtue. In other words, the literature of the day is weary of Revealed Religion.

5. Once more; that religion is in itself weariness is seen even in the conduct of the better sort of persons, who really on the whole are under the influence of its spirit. So dull and uninviting is calm and practical religion, that religious persons are ever exposed to the temptation of looking out for excitements of one sort or other, to make it pleasurable to them. The spirit of the Gospel is a meek, humble, gentle, unobtrusive spirit. It doth not cry nor lift up its voice in the streets, unless called upon by duty so to do, and then it does it with pain. Displays, pretension, conflict, are unpleasant to it.

What then is to be thought of persons who are ever on the search after novelties to make religion interesting to them; who seem to find that Christian activity cannot be kept up without unchristian party spirit, or Christian conversation without unchristian censoriousness? Why, this; that religion is to them as to others, taken by itself, weariness, and requires something foreign to its own nature to make it palatable. Truly it is a weariness to the natural man to serve God humbly and in obscurity; it is very wearisome, and very monotonous, to go on day after day watching all we do and think, detecting our secret failings, denying ourselves, creating within us, under God's grace, those parts of the Christian character in which we are deficient; wearisome to learn modesty, love of insignificance, willingness to be thought little of, backwardness to clear ourselves when slandered, and readiness to confess when we are wrong; to learn to have no cares for this world, neither to hope nor to fear, but to be resigned and contented!

I may close these remarks, by appealing to the consciences of all who have ever set about the work of religion in good earnest, whoever they may be, whether they have made less, or greater progress in their noble toil, whether they are matured saints, or feeble strugglers against the world and the flesh. They have ever confessed how great efforts were necessary to keep close to the commandments of God; in spite of their knowledge of the truth, and their faith, in spite of the aids and consolations they receive from above, still how often do their corrupt hearts betray them! Even their privileges are often burdensome to them, even to pray for the grace, which in Christ is pledged to them is an irksome task. They know that God's service is perfect freedom, and they are convinced, both in their reason and from their own experience of it, that it is true happiness; still they confess withal the strange reluctance of their nature to love their Maker and His Service. And this is the point in question; not only the mass of mankind, but also even the confirmed servants of Christ, witness to the opposition, which exists between their own nature and the demands of religion. This then is the remarkable fact, which I proposed to show. Can we doubt that man's will runs contrary to God's will—that the view which the inspired word takes of our present life, and of our destiny, does not satisfy us, as it rightly ought to do? That Christ hath neither form nor comeliness in our eyes; and though we see Him, we see no desirable beauty in Him? That holy, merciful, and meek Savior, the Eternal, the Only-begotten Son of God, our friend and infinite benefactor—He who left the glory of His Father and died for us, who has promised us the overflowing riches of His grace both here and hereafter. He is a light shining in a dark place, and "the darkness comprehendeth it not." "Light is come into the world and men love darkness rather than light."

The nature of man is flesh, and that which is born of the flesh is flesh, and ever must so remain; it never can discern, love, accept, the holy doctrines of the Gospel. It will occupy itself in various ways, it will take interest in things of sense and time, but it can never be religious. It is at enmity with God.
And now we see what must at once follow from what has been said. If our hearts are by nature set on the world for its own sake, and the world is one day to pass away, what are they to be set on, what to delight in, then? Say, how will the soul feel when, stripped of its present attire, which the world bestows, it stands naked and shuddering before the pure, tranquil, and severe majesty of the Lord its God, its most merciful, yet dishonored Maker and Savior? What are to be the pleasures of the soul in another life? Can they be the same as they are here? They cannot; Scripture tells us they cannot; the world passeth away—

now what is there left to love and enjoy through a long eternity? What a dark, forlorn, miserable eternity that will be!

It is then plain enough, though Scripture said not a word on the subject, that if we would be happy in the world to come, we must make us new hearts, and begin to love the things we naturally do not love. Viewing it as a practical point, the end of the whole matter is this, we must be changed; for we cannot, we cannot expect the system of the universe to come over to us; the inhabitants of heaven, the numberless creations of Angels, the glorious company of the Apostles, the goodly fellowship of the Prophets, the noble army of Martyrs, the holy Church universal, the Will and Attributes of God, these are fixed. We must go over to them. In our Savior's own authoritative words: "Verily, verily, except a man be born again, he cannot see the kingdom of God [2]." It is a plain matter of self-interest, to turn our thoughts to the means of changing our hearts, putting out of the question our duty towards God and Christ, our Savior and Redeemer.

"He hath no form nor comeliness, and when we see Him, there is no beauty that we should desire Him." It is not His loss that we love Him not, it is our loss. He is All blessed, whatever becomes of us. He is not less blessed because we are far from Him. It is we who are not blessed, except as we approach Him, except as we are like Him, except as we love Him. Woe unto us, if in the day in which He comes from Heaven we see nothing desirable or gracious in His wounds; but instead, have made for ourselves an ideal blessedness, different from that which will be manifested to us in Him. Woe unto us, if we have made pride, or selfishness, or the carnal mind, our standard of perfection and truth; if our eyes have grown dim, and our hearts gross, as regards the true light of men, and the glory of the Eternal Father. May He Himself save us from our self-delusions, whatever they are, and enable us to give up this world, that we may gain the next; —and to rejoice in Him, who had no home of His own, no place to lay His head, who was poor and lowly, and despised and rejected, and tormented and slain!

[1] Prov. xvii. 16.
[2] John iii. 3.

Reflection.

III. The World our Enemy. March 8, 1829

"We know that we are of God, and the whole world lieth in wickedness."—1 John v. 19.

Few words are of more frequent occurrence in the language of religion than "the world;" Holy Scripture makes continual mention of it, in the way of censure and caution; in the Service for Baptism it is described as one of three great enemies of our souls, and in the ordinary writings and conversation of Christians, I need hardly say, mention is made of it continually. Yet most of us, it would appear, have very indistinct notions what the world means. We know that the world is a something dangerous to our spiritual interests, and that it is in some way connected with human society—with men as a mixed multitude, contrasted with men one by one, in private and domestic life; but what it is, how it is our enemy, how it attacks, and how it is to be avoided, is not so clear.

Or if we conceive some distinct notion concerning it, still probably it is a wrong notion, —which leads us, in consequence, to misapply the Scripture precepts relating to the world; and this is even worse than overlooking them. I shall now, then, attempt to show what is meant by the world, and how, in consequence, we are to understand the information and warnings of the sacred writers concerning it.

1. Now, first, by the world is very commonly meant the present visible system of things, without taking into consideration whether it is good or bad. Thus St. John contrasts the world with the things that are in it, which are evil, "Love not the world, *neither* the things that are in the world [1]." Again, he presently says, "The world passeth away, *and* the lust thereof." Here, as in many other parts of Scripture, the world is not spoken of as actually sinful in itself (though its lusts are so, of course), but merely as some present visible system which is likely to

attract us, and is not to be trusted, because it cannot last. Let us first consider it in this point of view.

There is, as a matter of necessity, a great variety of stations and fortunes among mankind; hardly two persons are in the same outward circumstances, and possessed of the same mental resources. Men differ from each other, and are bound together into one body or system by the very points in which they differ; they depend on each other; such is the will of God. This system is the world, to which it is plain belong our various modes of supporting ourselves and families by exertion of mind and body, our intercourse with others, our duty towards others, the social virtues, —industry, honesty, prudence, justice, benevolence, and the like. These spring all from our present lot in life, and tend to our present happiness. This life holds out prizes to merit and exertion. Men rise above their fellows; they gain fame and honors, wealth and power, which we therefore call worldly goods. The affairs of nations, the dealings of people with people, the interchange of productions between country and country, are of this world. We are educated in boyhood for this world; we play our part on a stage more or less conspicuous, as the case may be; we die, we are no more, we are forgotten, as far as the present state of things is concerned; all this is of the world.

By the world, then, is meant this course of things, which we see carried on by means of human agency, with all its duties and pursuits. It is not necessarily a sinful system; rather it is framed, as I have said, by God Himself, and therefore cannot be otherwise than good. And yet even thus considering it, we are bid not to love the world: even in this sense the world is an enemy of our souls; and for this reason, because the love of it is dangerous to beings circumstanced as we are, —things in themselves good being not good to us sinners. And this state of things which we see, fair and excellent in itself, is very likely (for the very reason that it is seen, and because the spiritual and future world is not seen) to seduce our wayward hearts from our true and eternal good.

As the traveler on serious business may be tempted to linger, while he gazes on the beauty of the prospect which opens on his way, so this well-ordered and divinely-governed world, with all its blessings of sense and knowledge, may lead us to neglect those interests which will endure when itself has passed away. In truth, it promises more than it can fulfill. The goods of life and the applause of men have their excellence, and, as far as they so, are really good; but they are short-lived. And hence it is that many pursuits in themselves honest and right, are nevertheless to be engaged in with caution, lest they seduce us; and those perhaps with especial caution, which tend to the wellbeing of men in this life. The sciences, for instance, of good government, of acquiring wealth, of preventing and relieving want, and the like, are for this reason especially dangerous; for fixing, as they do, our exertions on this world as an end, they go far to persuade us that they have no other end; they accustom us to think too much of success in life and temporal prosperity; nay, they may even teach us to be jealous of religion and its institutions, as if these stood in our way, preventing us from doing so much for the worldly interests of mankind as we might wish.

In this sense it is that St. Paul contrasts sight and faith. We see this world; we only believe that there is a world of spirits, we do not see it: and inasmuch as sight has more power over us than belief, and the present than the future, so are the occupations and pleasures of this life injurious to our faith. Yet not, I say, in themselves sinful; as the Jewish system was a temporal system, yet divine, so is the system of nature—this world—divine, though temporal. And as the Jews became carnal-minded even by the influence of their divinely-appointed system, and thereby rejected the Savior of their souls; in like manner, men of the world are hardened by God's own good world, into a rejection of Christ. In neither case through the fault of the things which are seen, whether miraculous or providential, but accidentally, through the fault of the human heart.

2. But now, secondly, let us proceed to consider the world, not only as dangerous, but as positively sinful, according to the text—"the whole world lieth in wickedness." It was created well in all respects, but even before it as yet had fully grown out into its parts, while as yet the elements of human society did but lie hid in the nature and condition of the first man, Adam fell; and thus the world, with all its social ranks, and aims, and pursuits, and pleasures, and prizes, has ever from its birth been sinful. The infection of sin spread through the whole system, so that although the framework is good and divine, the spirit and life within it are evil. Thus, for instance, to be in a high station is the gift of God; but the pride and injustice to which it has given scope is from the Devil.

To be poor and obscure is also the ordinance of God; but the dishonesty and discontent, which are often seen in the poor, is from Satan. To cherish and protect wife and family is God's appointment; but the love of gain, and the low ambition, which lead many a man to exert himself, are sinful. Accordingly, it is said in the text, "The world lieth in wickedness,"—it is plunged and steeped, as it were, in a flood of sin, not a part of it remaining as God originally created it, not a part pure from the corruptions with which Satan has disfigured it.

Look into the history of the world, and what do you read there? Revolutions and changes without number, kingdoms rising and falling; and when without crime? States are established by God's ordinance, they have their existence in the necessity of man's nature, but when was one ever established, nay, or maintained, without war and bloodshed? Of all natural instincts, what is more powerful than that which forbids us to shed our fellows' blood? We shrink with natural horror from the thought of a murderer; yet not a government has ever been settled, or a state acknowledged by its neighbors, without war and the loss of life; nay, more than this, not content with unjustifiable bloodshed, the guilt of which must lie somewhere, instead of lamenting it as a grievous and humiliating evil, the world has chosen to honor the conqueror with its amplest share of admiration. To become a hero, in the eyes of the world, it is almost necessary to break the laws of God and man. Thus the deeds of the world are matched by the opinions and principles of the world: it adopts bad doctrine to defend bad practice; it loves darkness because its deeds are evil.

And as the affairs of nations are thus depraved by our corrupt nature, so are all the appointments and gifts of Providence perverted in like manner. What can be more excellent than the vigorous and patient employment of the intellect; yet in the hands of Satan it gives birth to a proud philosophy. When St. Paul preached, the wise men of the world, in God's eyes, were but fools, for they had used their powers of mind in the cause of error, their reasonings even led them to be irreligious and immoral; and they despised the doctrine of a resurrection which they neither loved nor believed. And again, all the more refined arts of life have been disgraced by the vicious tastes of those who excelled in them; often they have been consecrated to the service of idolatry; often they have been made the instruments of sensuality and riot.

But it would be endless to recount the manifold and complex corruption which man has introduced into the world which God made good, evil has preoccupied the whole of it, and holds fast its conquest. We know, indeed, that the gracious God revealed Himself to His sinful creatures very soon after Adam's fall. He showed His will to mankind again and again, and pleaded with them through many ages; till at length His Son was born into this sinful world in the form of man, and taught us how to please Him. Still, hitherto the good work has proceeded slowly: such is His pleasure. Evil had the start of good by many days; it filled the world, it holds it: it has the strength of possession, and if has its strength in the human heart; for though we cannot keep from approving what is right in our conscience, yet we love and encourage what is wrong; so that when evil was once set up in the world, it was secured in its seat by the unwillingness with which our hearts relinquish it.

And now I have described what is meant by the sinful world; that is, the world as corrupted by man, the course of human affairs viewed in its connexion with the principles, opinions, and practices that actually direct it. There is no mistaking these; they are evil; and of these it is that St. John says, "If any man love the world, the love of the Father is not in him. For all that is in the world, the lust of the flesh, and the lust of the eyes, and the pride of life, is not of the Father, but is of the world [2]."

The world then is the enemy of our souls; first, because, however innocent its pleasures, and praiseworthy its pursuits may be, they are likely to engross us, unless we are on our guard: and secondly, because in all its best pleasures, and noblest pursuits, the seeds of sin have been sown; an enemy hath done this; so that it is most difficult to enjoy the good without partaking of the evil also. As an orderly system of various ranks, with various pursuits and their several rewards, it is to be considered not sinful indeed, but dangerous to us. On the other hand, considered in reference to its principles and actual practices, it is really a sinful world.

Accordingly, when we are bid in Scripture to shun the world, it is meant that we must be cautious, lest we love what is good in it too well, and lest we love the bad at all. —However, there is a mistaken notion sometimes entertained, that the world is some particular set of persons, and that to shun the world is to shun them; as if we could point out, as it were, with the finger, what is the world, and thus could easily rid ourselves of one of our three great enemies. Men, who are beset with this notion, are often great lovers of the world notwithstanding, while they think themselves at a distance from it altogether. They love its pleasures, and they yield to its principles, yet they speak strongly against men of the world, and avoid them. They act the part of superstitious people, who are afraid of seeing evil spirits in what are considered haunted places, while these spirits are busy at their hearts instead, and they do not suspect it.

3. Here then is a question, which it will be well to consider, viz. how far the world is a separate body from the Church of God. The two are certainly contrasted in the text, as elsewhere in Scripture. "We know that we are of God, and *the whole world* lieth in wickedness." Now the true account of this is, that the Church so far from being literally, and in fact, separate from the wicked world, is within it. The Church is a body, gathered together in the world, and in a process of separation from it. The world's power, alas! Is over the Church, because the Church has gone forth into the world to save the world. All Christians are in the world, and of the world, so far as sin still has dominion over them; and not even the best of us is clean every whit from sin.

Though then, in our idea of the two, and in their principles, and in their future prospects, the Church is one thing, and the world is another, yet in present matter of fact, the Church is of the world, not separate from it; for the grace of God has but partial possession even of religious men, and the best that can be said of us is, that we have two sides, a light side and a dark, and that the dark happens to be the outermost. Thus we form part of the world to each other, though we be not of the world. Even supposing there were a society of men influenced individually by Christian motives, still this society, viewed as a whole, would be a worldly one, I mean a society holding and maintaining many errors, and countenancing many bad practices. Evil ever floats at the top. And if we inquire why it is that the good in Christians is seen less than the bad? I answer, first, because there is less of it; and secondly, because evil forces itself upon general notice, and good does not.

So that in a large body of men, each contributing his portion, evil displays itself on the whole conspicuously, and in all its diversified shapes. And thirdly, from the nature of things, the soul cannot be understood by any but God, and a religious spirit is in St. Peter's words, "the hidden man of the heart." It is only the actions of others which we see for the most part, and since there are numberless ways of doing wrong, and but one of doing right, and numberless ways too of regarding and judging the conduct of others, no wonder that even the better sort of men, much more the generality, are, and seem to be, so sinful. God only sees the circumstances under which a man acts, and why he acts in this way and not in that. God only sees perfectly the train of thought which preceded his action, the motive, and the reasons. And God alone (if aught is ill done, or sinfully) sees the deep contrition afterwards, —the habitual lowliness, then bursting forth into special self-reproach, —and the meek faith casting itself wholly upon God's mercy.

Think for a moment, how many hours in the day every man is left wholly to himself and his God, or rather how few minutes he is in intercourse with others —consider this, and you will perceive how it is that the life of the Church is hid with God, and how it is that the outward conduct of the Church must necessarily look like the world, even far more than it really is like it, and how vain, in consequence, the attempt is (which, some make) of separating the world distinctly from the Church. Consider, moreover, how much there is, while we are in the body, to stand in the way of one mind communicating with another. We are imprisoned in the body, and our intercourse is by means of words, which feebly represent our real feelings.

Hence the best motives and truest opinions are misunderstood, and the most sound rules of conduct misapplied by others. And Christians are necessarily more or less strange to each other; nay, and as far as the appearance of things is concerned, almost mislead each other, and are, as I have said, the world one to another. It is long, indeed, before we become at all acquainted with each other, and we appear the one to the other cold, or harsh, or capricious, or self-willed, when we are not so. So that it unhappily comes to pass, that even good men retire from each other into themselves, and to their God, as if retreating from the rude world.

And if all this takes place in the case of the better sort of men, how much more will it happen in the case of those multitudes who are still unstable in faith and obedience, half Christians, not having yet wrought themselves into any consistent shape of opinion and practice! These, so far from showing the better part of themselves, often affect to be worse even than they are. Though they have secret fears and misgivings, and God's grace pleads with their conscience, and seasons of seriousness follow, yet they are ashamed to confess to each other their own seriousness, and they ridicule religious men lest they should be themselves ridiculed.

And thus, on the whole, the state of the case is as follows: that if we look through mankind in order to find out who make up the world, and who do not, we shall find none who are not of the world; inasmuch as there are none who are not exposed to infirmity. So that if to shun the world is to shun some body of men so called, we must shun all men, nay, ourselves too—which is a conclusion, which means nothing at all.

But let us, avoiding all refinements which lead to a display of words only, not to the improvement of our hearts and conduct, let us set to work practically; and instead of attempting to judge of mankind on a large scale, and to settle deep questions, let us take what is close at hand and concerns ourselves, and make use of such knowledge as we can obtain. Are we tempted to neglect the worship of God for some temporal object? This is of the world, and not to be admitted. Are we ridiculed for our conscientious conduct? This again is a trial of the world, and to be withstood. Are we tempted to give too much time to our recreations; to be idling when we should be working; reading or talking when we should be busy in our temporal calling; hoping for impossibilities, or fancying ourselves in some different state of life from our own; over anxious of the good opinion of others; bent upon getting the credit of industry, honesty, and prudence? All these are temptations of this world. Are we discontented with our lot, or are we over attached to it, and fretful and desponding when God recalls the good He has given? This is to be worldly-minded.

Look not about for the world as some vast and gigantic evil far off—its temptations are close to you, apt and ready, suddenly offered and subtle in their address. Try to bring down the words of Scripture to common life, and to recognize the evil in which this world lies, in your own hearts.
When our Savior comes, He will destroy this world, even His own work, and much more the lusts of the world, which are of the evil one; then at length we must lose the world, even if we cannot bring ourselves to part with it now. And we shall perish with the world, if on that day its lusts are found within us. "The world passeth away, and the lust thereof, but he that doeth the will of God abideth for ever."
[1] 1 John ii. 15.
[2] John ii. 15, 16.

Reflection.

IV. The Praise of Men. March 15, 1829

"They loved the praise of men more than the praise of God."—John xii. 43.

This is spoken of the chief rulers of the Jews, who, though they believed in Christ's Divine mission, were afraid to confess Him, lest they should incur temporal loss and shame from the Pharisees. The censure passed by St. John on these persons is too often applicable to Christians at the present day; perhaps, indeed, there is no one among us who has not at some time or other fallen under it. We love the good opinion of the world more than the approbation of Him who created us, redeemed us, has regenerated us, and who still preserves to us the opportunity of preparing ourselves for His future presence. Such is too often the case with us. It is well we should be aware that it is so; it is well we should dwell upon it, and that we should understand and feel that it is wrong, which many men do not.

Now it is an obvious question, why is it wrong to love the praise of men? For it may be objected, that we are accustomed to educate the young by means of praise and blame; that we encourage them by kind words *from us*, that is, from man; and punish them for disobedience. If, then, it may be argued, it is right to regard the opinions of others concerning us in our youth, it cannot be in itself wrong to pay attention to it at any other period of life. This is true; but I do not say that the mere love of praise and fear of shame are evil: regard to the corrupt world's praise or blame, this is what is sinful and dangerous. St. John, in the text, implies that the praise of men was, at the time spoken of, in opposition to the praise of God. It must be wrong to prefer any thing to the will of God.

To seek praise is in itself as little wrong, as it is wrong to hope, and to fear, and to love, and to trust; all depends upon the object hoped, or feared, or loved, or trusted; to seek the praise of good men is not wrong, any more than to love or to reverence good men; only wrong when it is in excess, when it interferes with the exercise of love and reverence towards God. Not wrong while we look on good men singly as instruments and servants of God; or, in the words of Scripture, while "we glorify God in them[1]." But to seek the praise of bad men, is in itself as wrong as to love the company of bad men, or to admire them.

It is not, I say, merely the love of praise that is a sin, but love of the corrupt world's praise. This is the case with all our natural feelings and affections; they are all in themselves good, and implanted by God; they are sinful, because we have in us by nature a something more than them, viz. an evil principle which perverts them to a bad end. Adam, before his fall, felt, we may suppose, love, fear, hope, joy, dislike, as we do now; but then he felt them only when he ought, and as he ought; all was harmoniously tempered and rightly adjusted in his soul, which was at unity with itself. But, at the fall, this beautiful order and peace was broken up; the same passions remained, but their use and action were changed; they rushed into extremes, sometimes excessive, sometimes the reverse. Indignation was corrupted into wrath, self-love became selfishness, self-respect became pride, and emulation envy and jealousy. They were at variance with each other; pride struggled with self-interest, fear with desire. Thus his soul became a chaos, and needed a new creation. Moreover, as I have said, his affections were set upon unsuitable objects. The natural man looks to this world, the world is his god; faith, love, hope, joy, are not excited in his mind by things spiritual and divine, but by things seen and temporal.

Considering, then, that love of praise is not a bad principle in itself, it is plain that a parent may very properly teach his child to love his praise, and fear his blame, when that praise and blame are given in accordance with God's praise and blame, and made subservient to them. And, in like manner, if the world at large took a correct and religious view of things, then its praise and blame would in its place be valuable too. Did the world admire what God admires; did it account humility, for instance, a great virtue, and pride a great sin; did it condemn that spirit of self-importance and sensitiveness of disgrace, which calls itself a love of honor; did it think little of temporal prosperity, wealth, rank, grandeur, and power, did it condemn arrogant and irreverent disputing, the noisy, turbulent spirit of ambition, the love of war and conquest, and the perverse temper which leads to jealousy and hatred; did it prefer goodness and truth to gifts of the intellect; did it think little of quickness, wit, shrewdness, power of speech and general acquirements, and much of patience, meekness, gentleness, firmness, faith, conscientiousness, purity, forgiveness of injuries,— then there would be no sin in our seeking the world's praise; and though we still ought to love God's praise above all, yet we might love the praise of the world in its degree, for it would be nothing more nor less than the praise of good men. But since, alas! The contrary is the case, since the world (as Scripture tells us) "lieth in wickedness," and the principles and practices which prevail on all sides of us are not those which the All-holy God sanctions, we cannot lawfully seek the world's praise. We cannot serve two masters who are enemies the one to the other. We are forbidden to love the world or any thing that is of the world, for it is not of the Father, but passeth away.

This is the reason why it is wrong to pursue the world's praise; viz. because we cannot have it and God's praise too. And yet, as the pursuit of it is wrong, so is it common, —for this reason: because God is unseen, and the world is seen; because God's praise and blame are future, the world's are present; because God's praise and blame are inward, and come quietly and without keenness, whereas the world's are very plain and intelligible, and make themselves felt. Take, for instance, the case of the young, on (what is called) entering into life. Very many, indeed, there are, whether in a higher or lower station, who enter into the mixed society of others early; so early, that it might be thought they had hardly had time to acquire any previous knowledge of right and wrong, any standard of right and wrong, other than the world gives, any principles by which to fight against the world. And yet it cannot quite be so. Whatever is the first time persons hear evil, it is quite certain that good has been beforehand with them, and they have a something within them which tells them it is evil. And much more, if they have been blessed, as most men are, with the protection of parents, or the kind offices of teachers or of God's ministers, they generally have principles of duty more or less strongly imprinted on their minds; and on their first intercourse with strangers they are shocked or frighted at seeing the improprieties and sins, which are openly countenanced. Alas! there are persons, doubtless (though God forbid it should be the case with any here present!), whose consciences have been so early trained into forgetfulness of religious duties, that they can hardly, or cannot at all, recollect the time I speak of; the time when they acted with the secret feeling that God saw them, saw all they did and thought. I will not fancy this to be the case with any who hear me. Rather, there are many of you, in different ranks and circumstances, who have, and ever have had, general impressions on your minds of the claims which religion has on you, but, at the same time, have been afraid of acting upon them, afraid of the opinion of the world, of what others would say if you set about obeying your conscience.

Ridicule is a most powerful instrument in the hands of Satan, and it is most vividly felt by the young. If any one wishes to do his duty, it is most easy for the cold, the heartless, and the thoughtless, to find out harsh, or provoking, or ridiculous names to fix upon him. My brethren, so many of you as are sensitive of the laughter or contempt of the world, this is your cross; you must wear it, you must endure it patiently; it is the mark of your conformity to Christ; He despised the shame: you must learn to endure it, from the example and by the aid of your Savior. You must love the praise of God more than the praise of men. It is the very trial suited to you, appointed for you, to establish you in the faith. You are not tempted with gain or ambition, but with ridicule.

And be sure, that unless you withstand it, you cannot endure hardships as good soldiers of Jesus Christ, you will not endure other temptations which are to follow. How can you advance a step in your after and more extended course till the first difficulty is overcome? You need faith, and "a double-minded man," says St. James, "is unstable in all his ways." Moreover, be not too sure that all who show an inclination to ridicule you, feel exactly as they say. They speak with the loudest speaker; speak you boldly, and they will speak with you. They have very little of definite opinion themselves, or probably they even feel with you, though they speak against you. Very likely they have uneasy, unsatisfied consciences, though they seem to sin so boldly; and are as afraid of the world as you can be, nay, more so; they join in ridiculing you, lest others should ridicule them; or they do so in a sort of self-defense against the reproaches of their own consciences. Numbers in this bad world talk loudly against religion in order to encourage each other in sin, because they need encouragement.

They are cowards, and rely on each other for support against their fears. They know they ought to be other than they are, but are glad to avail themselves of any thing that looks like argument, to overcome their consciences withal. And ridicule is a kind of argument—such as it is; and numbers ridiculing together are a still stronger one—of the same kind. Anyhow, there are few indeed who will not feel afterwards, in times of depression or alarm, that you are right, and they themselves are wrong. Those who serve God faithfully have a friend of their own, in each man's bosom, witnessing for them; even in those who treat them ill. And I suppose no young person has been able, through God's mercy, to withstand the world's displeasure, but has felt at this time or that, that this is so, and in a little time will, with all humility, have the comfort of feeling it while he is withstanding the world.

But now supposing he has not had strength of mind to withstand the world; but has gone the way of the world. Suppose he has joined the multitude in saying and doing what he should not. We know the careless, thoughtless, profane habits which most men live in, making light of serious subjects, and being ashamed of godliness and virtue; ashamed of going to church regularly, ashamed of faith, ashamed of chastity, ashamed of innocence, ashamed of obedience to persons in authority. Supposing a person has been one of these, and then through God's grace repents. It often pleases God, in the course of His Providence, to rouse men to reflection by the occurrences of life. In such circumstances they certainly will have a severe trial to stand against the world.

Nothing is more painful in the case of such persons, than the necessity often imposed upon them of acting contrary to the opinion and wishes of those with whom they have till now been intimate, —whom they have admired and followed. Intimacies have already been formed, and ties drawn tight, which it is difficult to sever. What is the person in question to do? Rudely to break them at once? No. But is he to share in sins in which he formerly took part? No; whatever censure, contempt, or ridicule attaches to him in consequence.

But what, then, is he to do? His task, I say, is painful and difficult, but he must not complain, for it is his own making; it is the natural consequence of his past neglect of God. So much is plain, —he must abstain from all sinful actions; not converse lightly or irreverently where formerly he was not unwilling so to do; not spend his time, as heretofore, in idleness or riot; avoid places whither he is not called by actual duty, which offer temptation to sin; observe diligently attendance on church; not idle away the Lord's Day in vanity, or worse; not add to the number of his acquaintance any thoughtless persons. All this is quite plain, and in doing this I know he will incur the ridicule of his companions. He will have much to bear. He must bear to be called names, to be thought a hypocrite, to be thought to be affecting something out of the way, to be thought desirous of recommending himself to this or that person. He must be prepared for malicious and untrue reports about himself; many other trials must he look for. They are his portion.

He must pray God to enable him to bear them meekly. He must pray for himself, he must pray for those who ridicule him. He has deserved ridicule. He has nothing to boast of, if he bears it well. He has nothing to boast of that he incurs it. He has nothing to boast of, as if he were so much better than those who ridicule him; he was once as they are now. He is now just a little better than they are. He has just begun a new life. He has got a very little way in it, or rather no way, nothing beyond professing it; and he has the reproach of the world in consequence of his profession. Well, let him see to it that this reproach is not in vain, that he has a right to the reproach. Let him see to it that he acts as well as professes. It will be miserable indeed if he incurs the reproach, and yet does not gain the reward. Let him pray God to perfect in him what He has begun in him, and to begin and perfect it also in all those that reproach him. Let him pray for Christ's grace to bear hardships in Christ's spirit; to be able to look calmly in the world's face, and bear its frown; to trust in the Lord, and be doing good; to obey God, and so to be reproached, not for professing only, but for performing, not for doing nothing, but for doing something, and in God's cause.

If we are under reproach, let us have something to show for it. At present, such a one is but a child in the Gospel; but in time, St. Peter's words will belong to him, and he may appropriate them. "This is thankworthy, if a man for conscience towards God endure grief, suffering wrongfully. For what glory is it, if when ye be buffeted for your faults ye shall take it patiently? but if, when ye do well and suffer for it, ye take it patiently, this is acceptable with God."

What happens to the young in one way, and to penitent sinners in another, happens in one way or other to all of us. In the case of all of us occasions arise, when practices countenanced by others do not approve themselves to our consciences. If after serious thought we find we cannot acquiesce in them, we must follow our consciences, and stand prepared for the censure of others. We must submit (should it be unavoidable) to appear to those who have no means of understanding us, self-willed, or self-conceited, or obstinate, or eccentric, or headstrong, praying the while that God's mercy may vouchsafe to us, that we be not really what we seem to the world.

Some are exposed to a temptation of a different kind, that of making themselves seem more religious than they really are. It may happen, that to advocate right opinions may be profitable to our worldly interests, and be attended by the praise of men. You may ask, since in such cases God and man approve the same thing, why should the applause of the world be accounted dangerous then? I answer, it is dangerous because God requires of us a modest silence in our religion; but we cannot be religious in the eyes of men without displaying religion. I am now speaking of display. God sees our thoughts without our help, and praises *them*; but we cannot be praised by men without being seen by men: whereas often the very excellence of a religious action, according to our Savior's precept, consists in the not being seen by others. This is a frequent cause of hypocrisy in religion. Men begin by feeling as they should feel, then they think it a very hard thing that men should not know how well they feel, and in course of time they learn to speak without feeling. Thus they have learned to "love the praise of men more than the praise of God."—

We have to guard against another danger, against the mistake of supposing that the world's despising us is a proof that we are particularly religious; for this, too, is often supposed. Frequently it happens that we encumber our religion with extravagances, perversions, or mistakes, with which religion itself has no necessary connexion, and these, and not religion, excite the contempt of the world. So much is this the case, that the censure of numbers, or of the sober-minded, or of various and distinct classes of men, or censure consistently urged, or continued consistently, ought always to lead a man to be very watchful as to what he considers right to say or do in the line of duty, to lead him to examine his principles; to lead him, however thoroughly he adheres to these after all, to be unaffectedly humble about himself, and to convince him in matter of fact (what he might be quite sure of beforehand, from the nature of the case), that, however good his principles are in themselves, he is mixing up with them the alloy of his own frail and corrupt nature.

In conclusion, I would say to those who fear the world's censure, this: —

1. Recollect you cannot please all parties, you must disagree with some or other: you have only to choose (if you are determined to look to man) with which you will disagree. And, further, you may be sure that those who attempt to please all parties, please fewest; and that the best way to gain the world's good opinion (even if you were set upon this, which you must not be) is to show that you prefer the praise of God. Make up your mind to be occasionally misunderstood, and undeservedly condemned. You must, in the Apostle's words, go through evil report, and good report, whether on a contracted or a wider field of action. And you must not be anxious even for the praise of good men. To have, indeed, the approbation of those whose hearts are guided by God's Holy Spirit, is indeed much to be coveted. Still this is a world of discipline, not of enjoyment; and just as we are sometimes bound in duty to abstain from indulgences of sense in themselves innocent, so are we sometimes bound to deny ourselves the satisfaction derived from the praise even of the religious and conscientious. Only let us beware in all this, lest we act from pride and self-conceit.

2. In the next place, think of the multitude of beings, who, unseen themselves, may yet be surveying our conduct. St. Paul charges Timothy by the elect Angels [2]; and elsewhere he declares that the Apostles were made "a spectacle unto the world, and to Angels, and to men [3]." Are we then afraid to follow

what is right, lest the world should scoff? Rather let us be afraid not to follow it, because God sees us, and Christ, and the holy Angels. They rejoice over one sinner that repenteth; how must they mourn over those who fall away! What interest, surely, is excited among them, by the sight of the Christian's trial, when faith and the desire of the world's esteem are struggling in his heart for victory! What rejoicing if, through the grace of God, he overcomes! What sorrow and pity if he is overcome by the world! Accustom yourselves, then, to feel that you are on a public stage, whatever your station of life may be, that there are other witnesses to your conduct besides the world around you; and, if you feel shame of men, you should much more feel shame in the presence of God, and those servants of His that do His pleasure.

3. Still further: you fear the judgment of men upon you. What will you think of it on your deathbed? The hour must come, sooner or later, when your soul is to return to Him who gave it. Perhaps you will be sensible of your awful state. What will you then think of the esteem of the world? Will not all below seem to pass away, and be rolled up as a scroll, and the extended regions of the future solemnly set themselves before you? Then how vain will appear the applause or blame of creatures, such as we are, all sinners and blind judges, and feeble aids, and themselves destined to be judged for their deeds. When, then, you are tempted to dread the ridicule of man, throw your mind forward to the hour of death. You know what you will then think of it, if you are then able to think at all.

4. The subject is not exhausted. You fear shame; well, and will you not shrink from shame at the judgment-seat of Christ? There will be assembled all the myriads of men who ever lived, a vast multitude! There will be Apostles, prophets, martyrs, and all saints from the beginning of time. There will be all the good men you ever heard of or knew. There will be your own kindest and best friends, your pious parents, or brothers, or children. Now what think you of being put to shame before all these? You fear the contempt of one small circle of men; what think you of the Saints of God, of St. Mary, of St. Peter and St. Paul, of the ten thousand generations of mankind, being witnesses of your disgrace? You dread the opinion of those whom you do not love; but what if a father then shrink from a dear son, or the wife, or husband, your earthly companion, then tremble at the sight of you, and feel ashamed of you? Nay, there is One greater than parents, husbands, or brothers; One of whom you have been ashamed on earth; and what will He, that merciful, but neglected Savior, think of you then? Hear His own words: —"Whosoever shall be ashamed of

Me and of My words, of him shall the Son of Man be ashamed, when He shall come in His own glory, and in His Fathers, and of the holy Angels." Then such unhappy men, how will they feel shame at themselves! They will despise and loathe themselves; they will hate and abominate their own folly; they will account themselves brutish and mad, so to have been beguiled by the devil, and to have trifled with the season of mercy. "Many of them that sleep in the dust of the earth," says Daniel, "shall awake, some to everlasting life, and some to shame and everlasting contempt."

Let us, then, rouse ourselves, and turn from man to God; what have we to do with the world, we who from our infancy have been put on our journey heavenward? Take up your cross and follow Christ. He went through shame far greater than can be yours. Do you think He felt nothing when He was lifted up on the Cross to public gaze, amid the contempt and barbarous triumphings of His enemies, the Pharisees, Pilate and his Roman guard, Herod and his men of war, and the vast multitude collected from all parts of the world? They all looked on Him with hatred and insult, yet He endured (we are told), "despising the shame [4]." It is a high privilege to be allowed to be conformed to Christ; St. Paul thought it so, so have all good men.

The whole Church of God, from the days of Christ to the present, has been ever held in shame and contempt by men of this world. Proud men have reasoned against its Divine origin; crafty men have attempted to degrade it to political purposes: still it has lasted for many centuries; it will last still, through the promised help of God the Holy Ghost; and that same promise which is made to it first as a body, is assuredly made also to every one of us who seeks grace from God through it. The grace of our Lord and Savior is pledged to every one of us without measure, to give us all necessary strength and holiness when we pray for it; and Almighty God tells us Himself, "Fear ye not the reproach of men, neither be ye afraid of their revilings. For the moth shall eat them up like a garment, and the worm shall eat them like wool; but My righteousness shall be for ever, and My salvation from generation to generation."
[1] Gal. i. 24.
[2] 1 Tim. v. 21.
[3] 1 Cor. iv. 9.
[4] Heb. xii. 2.

Reflection.

V. The Duty of Self-Denial. March 28, 1830

"Surely I have behaved and quieted myself, as a child that is weaned of his mother: my soul is even as a weaned child."—Psalm cxxxi. 2.

Self-denial of some kind or other is involved, as is evident, in the very notion of renewal and holy obedience. To change our hearts is to learn to love things which we do not naturally love—to unlearn the love of this world; but this involves, of course, a thwarting of our natural wishes and tastes. To be righteous and obedient implies self-command; but to possess power we must have gained it; nor can we gain it without a vigorous struggle, a persevering warfare against ourselves. The very notion of being religious implies self-denial, because by nature we do not love religion.

Self-denial, then, is a subject never out of place in Christian teaching; still more appropriate is it at a time like this, when we have entered upon the forty days of Lent, the season of the year set apart for fasting and humiliation.
This indeed is not all that is meant by self-denial; but before proceeding with the subject, I would ask whether the generality of mankind go as far as this: it is plain that they do not. They do not go so far as to realize to themselves that religious obedience involves a thwarting of those wishes and inclinations which are natural to them. They do not like to be convinced; much less will they act upon the notion, that religion is difficult. You may hear men of the world say plainly, and as if in the way of argument, "that God will not punish us for indulging the passions with which we are born; that it is no praise to be unnatural; and no crime to be a man."

This, however, may seem an extreme case; yet are there not a great many decent and respectable men, as far as outward character goes, who at least fix their thoughts on worldly comfort, as the greatest of goods, and who labor to place themselves in easy circumstances, under the notion that, when they can retire from the business of their temporal calling, then they may (in a quiet, unexceptionable way of course) consult their own tastes and likings, take their pleasure, and indulge themselves in self-importance and self-satisfaction, in the enjoyment of wealth, power, distinction, popularity, and credit? I am not at this moment asking whether such indulgences are in themselves allowable or not, but whether the life which centers in them does not imply the absence of any very deep views of sanctification as a process, a change, a painful toil, of working out our own salvation with fear and trembling, of preparing to meet our God, and waiting for the judgment? You may go into mixed society; you will hear men conversing on their friend's prospects, openings in trade, or realized wealth, on his advantageous situation, the pleasant connexions he has formed, the land he has purchased, the house he has built; then they amuse themselves with conjecturing what this or that man's property may be, where he lost, where he gained, his shrewdness, or his rashness, or his good fortune in this or that speculation.

Observe, I do not say that such conversation is wrong, I do not say that we must always have on our lips the very thoughts which are deepest in our hearts, or that it is safe to judge of individuals by such speeches; but when this sort of conversation is the customary standard conversation of the world, and when a line of conduct answering to it is the prevalent conduct of the world (and this is the case), is it not a grave question for each of us, as living in the world, to ask himself what abiding notion we have of the necessity of self-denial, and how far we are clear of the danger of resembling that evil generation which "ate and drank, which married wives, and were given in marriage, which bought and sold, planted, and builded, till it rained fire and brimstone from heaven, and destroyed them all[1]?"

It is strange, indeed, how far this same forgetfulness and transgression of the duty of self-denial at present spreads. Take another class of persons, very different from those just mentioned, men who profess much love for religion— I mean such as maintain, that if a man has faith he will have works without his trouble, so that he need be at no pains about performing them. Such persons at best seem to say, that religious obedience is to follow as a matter of course, an easy work, or rather a necessary consequence, from having some strong urgent motive, or from some bright vision of the Truth acting on the mind; and thus they dismiss from their religion the notion of self-denial, or the effort and warfare of faith against our corrupt natural will, whether they actually own that they dismiss it or not. I say that they do this at best, for it often happens, as I just now intimated, that they actually avow their belief that faith is all-sufficient, and do not let their minds dwell at all on the necessity of works of righteousness. All this being considered, surely I am not wrong in saying that the notion of self-denial as a distinct religious duty, and, much more (as it may well be called), the essence of religious obedience, is not admitted into the minds of the generality of men.

But let it be observed, I have hitherto spoken of self-denial not as a distinct duty actually commanded in Scripture, but merely as it is involved in the very notion of sanctification, as necessarily attendant on that change of nature which God the Holy Spirit vouchsafes to work within us. But now let us consider it in the light of the Scripture precepts concerning it, and we shall come to a still more serious view of it, serious (I mean) to those who are living to the world; it is this, —that it is our duty, not only to deny ourselves in what is sinful, but even, in a certain measure, in lawful things, to keep a restraint over ourselves even in innocent pleasures and enjoyments.

Now the first proof I shall give of this will at the same time explain what I mean.

Fasting is clearly a Christian duty, as our Savior implies in His Sermon on the Mount. Now what is fasting but a refraining from what is lawful; not merely from what is sinful, but what is innocent? —from that bread which we might lawfully take and eat with thanksgiving, but which at certain times we do not take, in order to deny ourselves. Such is Christian self-denial,—not merely a mortification of what is sinful, but an abstinence even from God's blessings.

Again: consider the following declaration of our Savior: He first tells us, "Strait is the gate, and narrow is the way which leadeth unto life, and few there be that find it." And again: "Strive to enter in, for many, I say unto you, will seek (only seek) to enter in, and shall not be able." Then He explains to us what this peculiar difficulty of a Christian's life consists in: "If any man come to Me, and hate not his father, and mother, and wife, and children, and brethren, and sisters, yea, and his own life also, he cannot be My disciple [2]." Now whatever is precisely meant by this (which I will not here stop to inquire), so far is evident, that our Lord enjoins a certain refraining, not merely from sin, but from innocent comforts and enjoyments of this life, or a self-denial in things lawful.

Again, He says, "If any man will come after Me, let him deny himself, and take up his cross daily, and follow Me [3]." Here He shows us from His own example what Christian self-denial is. It is taking on us a cross after His pattern, not a mere refraining from sin, for He had no sin, but a giving up what we might lawfully use. This was the peculiar character in which Christ came on earth. It was this spontaneous and exuberant self-denial which brought Him down. He who was one with God, took upon Him our nature, and suffered death—and why? to save us whom He needed not save. Thus He denied Himself, and took up His cross. This is the very aspect, in which God, as revealed in Scripture, is distinguished from that exhibition of His glory, which nature gives us: power, wisdom, love, mercy, long-suffering—these attributes, though far more fully and clearly displayed in Scripture than in nature, still are in their degree seen on the face of the visible creation; but self-denial, if it may be said, this incomprehensible attribute of Divine Providence, is disclosed to us only in Scripture. "God so loved the world that He gave His Son[4]." Here is self-denial. And the Son of God so loved us, that "though He was rich yet for our sakes He became poor [5]." Here is our Savior's self-denial. "He pleased not Himself."

And what Christ did when He came on earth, that have all His saints done both before and since His coming. Even the saints of the Old Testament so conducted themselves, to whom a temporal promise was made, and who, if any, might have surrendered themselves to the enjoyment of it. They had a temporal promise, they had a present reward; yet, with a noble faith, and a largeness of soul (how they put us to shame who have so much higher privileges!) the Jewish believers grudged themselves the milk and honey of Canaan, as seeking a better country, that is a heavenly. Elijah, how unlike is he to one who had a temporal promise! Or take again the instance of Daniel, which is still more striking, —"They that wear soft clothing are in kings' houses." Daniel was first in power in the palace of the greatest monarchs of his time. Yet what do we read of him? First of his living upon pulse and water, afterwards of his fasting in sackcloth and ashes, at another time of his mourning three full weeks, eating no pleasant bread, neither flesh nor wine coming in his mouth, nor anointing himself at all, till those three weeks were fulfilled. Can any thing more clearly show the duty of self-denial, even in lawful things, in the case of Christians, when even God's servants, before Christ came and commanded it, in proportion as they had evangelical gifts, observed it?

Or again, consider the words of the text spoken by David, who, if any, had riches and power poured upon him by the hand of God. He says, he has "behaved and quieted" himself lest he should be proud, and made himself "as a weaned child." What an impressive word is "weaned!" David had put away the unreserved love and the use of this world. We naturally love the world, and innocently; it is before us, and meets our eyes and hands first; its pleasures are dear to us, and many of them not in themselves sinful, only in their excess, and some of them not sinful at all;—those, for instance, which we derive from our home, our friends, and our prospects, are the first and natural food of our mind.

But as children are weaned from their first nourishment, so must our souls put away childish things, and be turned from the pleasures of earth to those of heaven; we must learn to compose and quiet ourselves as a weaned child, to put up with the loss of what is dear to us, nay, voluntarily to give it up for Christ's sake.

Much more after Christ came does St. Paul give us this same lesson in the ninth chapter of his first Epistle to the Corinthians: "Every one that striveth for the mastery is temperate in all things," i. e. has power over himself, and keeps himself in subjection, as he presently says. Again, in the seventh chapter, "The time is short; it remaineth that both they that have wives be as though they had none, and they that weep as though they wept not, and they that rejoice as though they rejoiced not, and they that buy as though they possessed not, and they that use this world as not abusing it." Here the same doctrine of moderation or temperance in lawful indulgences is strongly enforced; to weep, to rejoice, to buy, to possess, to marry, to use this world, are not unlawful, yet we must not use God's earthly gifts to the full, but in all things we must be self-denying.
Such is Christian self-denial, and it is incumbent upon us for many reasons. The Christian denies himself in things lawful because he is aware of his own weakness and liability to sin; he dares not walk on the edge of a precipice; instead of going to the extreme of what is allowable, he keeps at a distance from evil, that he may be safe. He abstains lest he should not be temperate; he fasts lest he should eat and drink with the drunken. As is evident, many things are in themselves right and unexceptionable which are inexpedient in the case of a weak and sinful creature: his case is like that of a sick person; many kinds

of food, good for a man in health, are hurtful when he is ill—wine is poison to a man in a fierce fever. And just so, many acts, thoughts, and feelings, which would have been allowable in Adam before his fall, are prejudicial or dangerous in man fallen. For instance, anger is not sinful in itself. St. Paul implies this, when he says, "Be ye angry and sin not [6]." And our Savior on one occasion is said to have been angry, and He was sinless. Almighty God, too, is angry with the wicked. Anger, then, is not in itself a sinful feeling; but in man, constituted as he is, it is so highly dangerous to indulge it, that self-denial here is a duty from mere prudence. It is almost impossible for a man to be angry only so far as he ought to be; he will exceed the right limit, his anger will degenerate into pride, sullenness, malice, cruelty, revenge, and hatred. It will inflame his diseased soul, and poison it. Therefore, he must abstain from it, as if it were *in itself* a sin (though it is not), for it is practically such to him.

Again, the love of praise is in itself an innocent passion, and might be indulged, were the world's opinion right and our hearts sound; but, as things are, human applause, if listened to, will soon make us forget how weak and sinful we are; so we must deny ourselves, and accept the praise even of good men, and those we love, cautiously and with reserve.

So, again, love of power is commonly attendant on a great mind; but he is the greatest of a sinful race who refrains himself, and turns from the temptation of it; for it is at once unbecoming and dangerous in a son of Adam. "Whosoever will be great among you, let him be your minister," says our Lord; "and whosoever will be chief among you, let him be your servant [7]." His reward will be hereafter; to reign with Christ, to sit down with Him on His throne, to judge angels, —yet without pride.

Again, even in affection towards our relations and friends, we must be watchful over ourselves, lest it seduce us from the path of duty. Many a father, from a kind wish to provide well for his family, neglects his own soul. Here, then, is a fault; not that we can love our relations too well, but that that strong and most praiseworthy affection for them may, accidentally, ensnare and corrupt our weak nature.

These considerations will show us the meaning of our Savior's words already cited, about the duty of hating our friends. To hate is to feel that perfect distaste for an object, that you wish it put away and got rid of; it is to turn away from it, and to blot out the thought of it from your mind. Now this is just the feeling we must cherish towards all earthly blessings, so far as Christ does not cast His light upon them. He (blessed be His name) has sanctioned and enjoined love and care for our relations and friends: Such love is a great duty; but should at any time His guidance lead us by a strange way, and the light of His providence pass on, and cast these objects of our earthly affection into the shade, then they must be at once in the shade to *us*, —they must, for the time, disappear from our hearts. "He that loveth father or mother more than Me, is not worthy of Me." So He says; and at such times, though still loving them, we shall seem to hate them; for we shall put aside the thought of them, and act as if they did not exist. And in this sense an ancient and harsh proverb is true: we must always so love our friends as feeling that one day or other we may perchance be called upon to hate them, —that is, forget them in the pursuit of higher duties.

Here, again, then, is an instance of self-denial in lawful things; and if a person says it is painful thus to feel, and that it checks the spontaneous and continual flow of love towards our friends to have this memento sounding in our ears, we must boldly acknowledge that it is painful. It is a sad thought, not that we can ever be called upon actually to put away the love of them, but to have to act as if we did not love them,—as Abraham when called on to slay his son. And this thought of the uncertainty of the future, doubtless, does tinge all our brightest affections (as far as this world is concerned) with a grave and melancholy hue. We need not shrink from this confession, remembering that this life is not our rest or happiness; —"*that* remaineth" to come. This sober chastised feeling is the very temper of David, when he speaks of having composed and quieted his soul, and weaned it from the babe's nourishment which this world supplies.

I hope I have made it clear, by these instances, what is meant by Christian self-denial. If we have good health, and are in easy circumstances, let us beware of high-mindedness, self-sufficiency, self-conceit, arrogance; of delicacy of living, indulgences, luxuries, comforts. Nothing is so likely to corrupt our hearts, and to seduce us from God, as to surround ourselves with comforts, —to have things our own way, —to be the centre of a sort of world, whether of things animate or inanimate, which minister to us. For then, in turn, we shall depend on them; they will become necessary to us; their very service and adulation will lead us to trust ourselves to them, and to idolize them. What examples are there in Scripture of soft luxurious men! Was it Abraham before the Law, who wandered through his days, without a home? or Moses, who gave the Law, and died in the wilderness? Or David under the Law, who "had no proud looks," and was "as a weaned child?" or the Prophets, in the latter days

48

of the Law, who wandered in sheepskins and goatskins? Or the Baptist, when the Gospel was superseding it, who was clad in raiment of camel's hair, and ate the food of the wilderness?

Or the Apostles, who were "the off scouring of all things"? Or our blessed Savior, who "had not a place to lay His head"? Who are the soft luxurious men in Scripture? There was the rich man, who "fared sumptuously every day," and then "lifted up his eyes in hell, being in torments." There was that other, whose "ground brought forth plentifully," and who said, "Soul, thou hast much goods laid up for many years;" and his soul was required of him that night. There was Demas, who forsook St. Paul, "having loved this present world." And, alas!

There was that highly-favored, that divinely-inspired king, rich and wise Solomon, whom it availed nothing to have measured the earth, and numbered its inhabitants, when in his old age he "loved many strange women," and worshipped their gods.

Far be it from us, soldiers of Christ, thus to perplex ourselves with this world, who are making our way towards the world to come. "No man that warreth, entangleth himself with the affairs of this life, that he may please Him who hath chosen him to be a soldier. If a man also strive for masteries, yet is he not crowned, except he strive lawfully." This is St. Paul's rule, as has already been referred to: accordingly, in another place, he bears witness of himself that he "died daily." Day by day he got more and more dead to this world; he had fewer ties to earth, a larger treasure in heaven. Nor let us think that it is over-difficult to imitate him, though we be not Apostles, nor are called to any extraordinary work, nor are enriched with any miraculous gifts: he would have all men like himself, and all may be like him, according to their place and measure of grace. If we would be followers of the great Apostle, first let us with him fix our eyes upon Christ our Savior; consider the splendor and glory of His holiness, and try to love it. Let us strive and pray that the love of holiness may be created within our hearts; and then acts will follow, such as befit us and our circumstances, in due time, without our distressing ourselves to find what they should be. You need not attempt to draw any precise line between what is sinful and what is only allowable: look up to Christ, and deny yourselves every thing, whatever its character, which you think He would have you relinquish. You need not calculate and measure, if you love much: you need not perplex yourselves with points of curiosity, if you have a heart to venture after Him. True, difficulties will sometimes arise, but they will be seldom. He bids you take up your cross; therefore accept the daily opportunities which occur of yielding to others, when you need not yield, and of doing unpleasant services, which you might avoid. He bids those who would be highest, live as the lowest: therefore, turn from ambitious thoughts, and (as far as you religiously may) make resolves against taking on you authority and rule. He bids you sell and give alms; therefore, hate to spend money on yourself.

Shut your ears to praise, when it grows loud: set your face like a flint, when the world ridicules, and smile at its threats. Learn to master your heart, when it would burst forth into vehemence, or prolong a barren sorrow, or dissolve into unseasonable tenderness. Curb your tongue, and turn away your eye, lest you fall into temptation. Avoid the dangerous air which relaxes you, and brace yourself upon the heights. Be up at prayer "a great while before day," and seek the true, your only Bridegroom, "by night on your bed." So shall self-denial become natural to you, and a change come over you, gently and imperceptibly; and, like Jacob, you will lie down in the waste, and will soon see Angels, and a way opened for you into heaven.

[1] Luke xvii. 27-29.
[2] Matt. vii. 14. Luke xiii. 24; xiv. 26.
[3] Luke ix. 23.
[4] John iii. 16.
[5] 2 Cor. viii. 9.
[6] Eph. iv. 26.
[7] Matt. xx. 26, 27

Reflection.

VI. The Lapse of Time. January 1, 1832

"Whatsoever thy hand findeth to do, do it with thy might; for there is no work, nor device, nor knowledge, nor wisdom, in the grave, whither thou goest."— Eccles. ix. 10.

Solomon's advice that we should do whatever our hand findeth to do with our might, naturally directs our thoughts to that great work in which all others are included, which will outlive all other works, and for which alone we really are placed here below—the salvation of our souls. And the consideration of this great work, which must be done with all our might, and completed before the grave, whither we go, presents itself to our minds with especial force at the commencement of a new year. We are now entering on a fresh stage of our life's journey; we know well how it will end, and we see where we shall stop in the evening, though we do not see the road. And we know in what our business lies while we travel, and that it is important for us to do it with our "might; for there is no work, nor device, nor knowledge, nor wisdom, in the grave." This is so plain, that nothing need be said in order to convince us that it is true. We know it well; the very complaint which numbers commonly make when told of it, is that they know it already, that it is nothing new, that they have no need to be told, and that it is tiresome to hear the same thing said over and over again, and impertinent in the person who repeats it. Yes; thus it is that sinners silence their conscience, by quarrelling with those who appeal to it; they defend themselves, if it may be called a defense, by pleading that they already know what they should do and do not, that they know perfectly well that they are living at a distance from God, and are in peril of eternal ruin; that they know they are making themselves children of Satan, and denying the Lord that bought them, and want no one to tell them so. Thus they witness against themselves.

However, though we already know well enough that we have much to do before we die, yet (if we will but attend) it may be of use to hear the fact dwelt upon; because by thinking over it steadily and seriously, we may possibly, through God's grace, gain some deep conviction of it; whereas while we keep to general terms, and confess that this life is important and is short, in the mere summary way in which men commonly confess it, we have, properly speaking, no knowledge of that great truth at all.

Consider, then, what it is to die; "there is no work, device, knowledge, or wisdom, in the grave." Death puts an end absolutely and irrevocably to all our plans and works, and it is inevitable. The Psalmist speaks to "high and low, rich and poor, one with another." "No man can deliver his brother, nor make agreement unto God for him." Even "wise men die, as well as the ignorant and foolish, and leave their riches for other [1]." Difficult as we may find it to bring it home to ourselves, to realize it, yet as surely as we are here assembled together, so surely will every one of us, sooner or later, one by one, be stretched on the bed of death. We naturally shrink from the thought of death, and of its attendant circumstances; but all that is hateful and fearful about it will be fulfilled in our case, one by one. But all this is nothing compared with the consequences implied in it. Death stops us; it stops our race. Men are engaged about their work, or about their pleasure; they are in the city, or the field; anyhow they are stopped; their deeds are suddenly gathered in—a reckoning is made—all is sealed up till the great day. What a change is this! In the words used familiarly in speaking of the dead, they are no more. They were full of schemes and projects; whether in a greater or humbler rank, they had their hopes and fears, their prospects, their pursuits, their rivalries; all these are now come to an end. One builds a house, and its roof is not finished; another buys merchandise, and it is not yet sold. And all their virtues and pleasing qualities which endeared them to their friends are, as far as this world is concerned, vanished. Where are they who were so active, so sanguine, so generous? The amiable, the modest, and the kind? We were told that they were dead; they suddenly disappeared; that is all we know about it. They were silently taken from us; they are not met in the seat of the elders, nor in the assemblies of the people, in the mixed concourse of men, nor in the domestic retirement that they prized.

As Scripture describes it, "the wind has passed over them, and they are gone, and their place shall know them no more." And they have burst the many ties that held them; they were parents, brothers, sisters, children, and friends; but the bond of kindred is broken, and the silver cord of love is loosed. They have been followed by the vehement grief of tears, and the long sorrow of aching hearts; but they make no return, they answer not; they do not even satisfy our wish to know that they sorrow for us as we for them. We talk about them thenceforth as if they were persons we do not know; we talk about them as third persons; whereas they used to be always with us, and every other thought which was within us was shared by them. Or perhaps, if our grief is too deep, we do not mention their names at all. And their possessions, too, all fall to others. The world goes on without them; it forgets them. Yes, so it is; the world contrives to forget that men have souls; it looks upon them all as mere parts of some great visible system. This continues to move on; to this the world ascribes a sort of life and personality. When one or other of its members die, it considers them only as falling out of the system, and as come to naught. For a minute, perhaps, it thinks of them in sorrow, then leaves them—leaves them forever. It keeps its eye on things seen and temporal. Truly whenever a man dies, rich or poor, an immortal soul passes to judgment; but somehow we read of the deaths of persons we have seen or heard of, and this reflection never comes across us.

Thus does the world really cast off men's souls, and recognizing only their bodies, it makes it appear as if "that which befalleth the sons of men befalleth beasts, even one thing befalleth them, as the one dieth so dieth the other; yea, they have all one breath, so that a man hath no pre-eminence over a beast, for all is vanity [2]."

But let us follow the course of a soul thus casting off the world, and cast off by it. It goes forth as a stranger on a journey. Man seems to die and to be no more, when he is but quitting us, and is really beginning to live. Then he sees sights which before it did not even enter into his mind to conceive, and the world is even less to him than he to the world. Just now he was lying on the bed of sickness, but in that moment of death what an awful change has come over him! What a crisis for him! There is stillness in the room that lately held him; nothing is doing there, for he is gone, he now belongs to others; he now belongs entirely to the Lord who bought him; to Him he returns; but whether to be lodged safely in His place of hope, or to be imprisoned against the great Day, that is another matter, that depends on the deeds done in the body, whether good or evil. And now what are his thoughts? How infinitely important now appears the value of time, now when it is nothing to him! Nothing; for though he spend centuries waiting for Christ, he cannot now alter his state from bad to good, or from good to bad. What he dieth that he must be forever; as the tree falleth so must it lie. This is the comfort of the true servant of God, and the misery of the transgressor. His lot is cast once and for all, and he can but wait in hope or in dread. Men on their death-beds have declared, that no one could form a right idea of the value of time till he came to die; but if this has truth in it, how much more truly can it be said after death! What an estimate shall we form of time while we are waiting for judgment! Yes, it is we—all this, I repeat, belongs to us most intimately. It is not to be looked at as a picture, as a man might read a light book in a leisure hour. *We* must die, the youngest, the healthiest, the most thoughtless; *we* must be thus unnaturally torn in two, soul from body; and only united again to be made more thoroughly happy or to be miserable for ever.

Such is death considered in its inevitable necessity, and its unspeakable importance—nor can we ensure to ourselves any certain interval before its coming. The time may be long; but it may also be short. It is plain, a man may die any day; all we can say is, that it is unlikely that he will die. But of this, at least, we are certain, that, come it sooner or later, death is continually on the move towards us. We are ever nearer and nearer to it. Every morning we rise we are nearer that grave in which there is no work, nor device, than we were.

We are now nearer the grave, than when we entered this Church. Thus life is ever crumbling away under us. What should we say to a man, who was placed on some precipitous ground, which was ever crumbling under his feet, and affording less and less secure footing, yet was careless about it? Or what should we say to one who suffered some precious liquor to run from its receptacle into the thoroughfare of men, without a thought to stop it? Who carelessly looked on and saw the waste of it, becoming greater and greater every minute? But what treasure can equal time? It is the seed of eternity: yet we suffer ourselves to go on, year after year, hardly using it at all in God's service, or thinking it enough to give Him at most a tithe or a seventh of it, while we strenuously and heartily sow to the flesh, that from the flesh we may reap corruption. We try how little we can safely give to religion, instead of having the grace to give abundantly. "Rivers of water run down mine eyes, because men keep not Thy law," so says the holy Psalmist. Doubtless an inspired prophet saw far more clearly than we can see, the madness of men in squandering that treasure upon sin, which is meant to buy their chief good; —but if so, what must this madness appear in God's sight! What an inveterate malignant evil is it in the hearts of the sons of men, that thus leads them to sit down to eat, and drink, and rise up to play, when time is hurrying on and judgment coming? We have been told what He thinks of man's unbelief, though we cannot enter into the depths of His thoughts. He showed it to us in act and deed, as far as we could receive it, when He even sent His Only-begotten Son into the world as at this time, to redeem us from the world, —which, most surely, was not lightly done; and we also learn His thoughts about it from the words of that most merciful Son, —which most surely were not lightly spoken, "The wicked," He says, "shall go into everlasting punishment."

Oh that there was such a heart in us that we would fear God and keep His commandments always! But it is of no use to speak; men know their duty— they will not do it. They say they do not need or wish to be told it, that it is an intrusion, and a rudeness, to tell them of death and judgment. So must it be, — and we, who have to speak to them, must submit to this. Speak we must, as an act of duty to God, whether they will hear, or not, and then must leave our words as a witness. Other means for rousing them we have none. We speak from Christ our gracious Lord, their Redeemer, who has already pardoned them freely, yet they will not follow Him with a true heart; and what can be done more?

Every year is open to us; it speaks to the thoughtful, and is heard by those, who have expectant ears, and watch for Christ's coming. The former year is gone, it is dead, there it lies in the grave of past time, not to decay however, and be forgotten, but kept in the view of God's omniscience, with all its sins and errors irrevocably written, till, at length, it will be raised again to testify about us at the last day; and who among us can bear the thought of his own doings, in the course of it? —All that he has said and done, all that has been conceived within his mind, or been acted on, and all that he has not said and done, which it was a duty to say or do. What a dreary prospect seems to be before us, when we reflect that we have the solemn word of truth pledged to us, in the last and most awful revelation, which God has made to us about the future, that in that day, the books will be opened, "and another book opened, which is the book of life, and the dead judged out of those things which were written in the books according to their works [3]!" What would a man give, any one of us, who has any real insight into his polluted and miserable state, what would he give to tear away some of the leaves there preserved! For how heinous are the sins therein written! Think of the multitude of sins done by us since we first knew the difference between right and wrong. We have forgotten them, but there we might read them clearly recorded. Well may holy David exclaim, "Remember not the sins of my youth nor my transgressions, according to Thy mercy remember Thou me." Conceive, too, the multitude of sins which have so grown into us as to become part of us, and in which we now live, not knowing, or but partially knowing, that they are sins, habits of pride, self-reliance, self-conceit, sullenness, impurity, sloth, selfishness, worldliness. The history of all these, their beginnings, and their growth, is recorded in those dreadful books; and when we look forward to the future, how many sins shall we have committed by this time next year, —though we try ever so much to know our duty, and overcome ourselves! Nay, or rather shall we have the opportunity of obeying or disobeying God for a year longer? Who knows whether by that time our account may not be closed forever?

"Remember me, O Lord, when Thou comest into Thy kingdom [4]." Such was the prayer of the penitent thief on the Cross, such must be our prayer. Who can do us any good, but He, who shall also be our Judge? When shocking thoughts about ourselves come across us and afflict us, "Remember me," this is all we have to say. We have "no work, nor device, nor knowledge, nor wisdom" of our own, to better ourselves withal. We can say nothing to God in defense of ourselves, —we can but acknowledge that we are grievous sinners, and addressing Him as suppliants, merely beg Him to bear us in mind in mercy, for His Son's sake to do us some favor, not according to our deserts, but for the love of Christ. The more we try to serve Him here, the better; but after all, so far do we fall short of what we should be, that if we had but what we are in ourselves to rely upon, wretched are we, —and we are forced out of ourselves by the very necessity of our condition. To whom should we go? Who can do us any good, but He who was born into this world for our regeneration, was bruised for our iniquities, and rose again for our justification? Even though we have served Him from our youth up, though after His pattern we have grown, as far as mere man can grow, in wisdom as we grew in stature, though we ever have had tender hearts, and a mortified will, and a conscientious temper, and an obedient spirit; yet, at the very best, how much have we left undone, how much done, which ought to be otherwise! What He can do for our nature, in the way of sanctifying it, we know indeed in a measure; we know, in the case of His saints; and we certainly do not know the limit of His carrying forward in those objects of His special favor the work of purification, and renewal through His Spirit. But for ourselves, we know full well that much as we may have attempted, we have done very little, that our very best service is nothing worth, —and the more we attempt, the more clearly we shall see how little we have hitherto attempted.

Those whom Christ saves are they who at once attempt to save themselves, yet despair of saving themselves; who aim to do all, and confess they do naught; who are all love, and all fear, who are the most holy, and yet confess themselves the most sinful; who ever seek to please Him, yet feel they never can; who are full of good works, yet of works of penance. All this seems a contradiction to the natural man, but it is not so to those whom Christ enlightens. They understand in proportion to their illumination, that it is possible to work out their salvation, yet to have it wrought out for them, to fear and tremble at the thought of judgment, yet to rejoice always in the Lord, and hope and pray for His coming.
[1] Ps. xlix. 2-10.

[2] Eccles. iii. 19.
[3] Rev. xx. 12.
[4] Luke xxiii. 42.

Reflection.

VII. The Season of Epiphany. January 17, 1841

"This beginning of miracles did Jesus in Cana of Galilee, and manifested forth His glory; and His disciples believed on Him."—John ii. 11.

The Epiphany is a season especially set apart for adoring the glory of Christ. The word may be taken to mean the manifestation of His glory, and leads us to the contemplation of Him as a King upon His throne in the midst of His court, with His servants around Him, and His guards in attendance. At Christmas we commemorate His grace; and in Lent His temptation; and on Good Friday His sufferings and death; and on Easter Day His victory; and on Holy Thursday His return to the Father; and in Advent we anticipate His second coming. And in all of these seasons He does something, or suffers something: but in the Epiphany and the weeks after it, we celebrate Him, not as on His field of battle, or in His solitary retreat, but as an august and glorious King; we view Him as the Object of our worship. Then only, during His whole earthly history, did He fulfill the type of Solomon, and held (as I may say) a court, and received the homage of His subjects; viz. when He was an infant. His throne was His undefiled Mother's arms; His chamber of state was a cottage or a cave; the worshippers were the wise men of the East, and they brought presents, gold, frankincense, and myrrh. All around and about Him seemed of earth, except to the eye of faith; one note alone had He of Divinity. As great men of this world are often plainly dressed, and look like other men, all but as having some one costly ornament on their breast or on their brow; so the Son of Mary in His lowly dwelling, and in an infant's form, was declared to be the Son of God Most High, the Father of Ages, and the Prince of Peace, by His star; a wonderful appearance which had guided the wise men all the way from the East, even unto Bethlehem.

This being the character of this Sacred Season, our services throughout it, as far as they are proper to it, are full of the image of a king in his royal court, of a sovereign surrounded by subjects, of a glorious prince upon a throne. There is no thought of war, or of strife, or of suffering, or of triumph, or of vengeance connected with the Epiphany, but of august majesty, of power, of prosperity, of splendor, of serenity, of benignity. Now, if at any time, it is fit to say, "The Lord is in His holy temple, let all the earth keep silence before Him [1]." "The Lord sitteth above the water flood, and the Lord remaineth a king for ever." "The Lord of Hosts is with us; the God of Jacob is our refuge." "O come, let us worship, and fall down, and kneel before the Lord our Maker." "O magnify the Lord our God, and fall down before His footstool, for He is Holy." "O worship the Lord in the beauty of holiness; bring presents, and come into His courts." I said that at this time of year the portions of our services which are proper to the season are of a character to remind us of a king on his throne, receiving the devotion of his subjects. Such is the narrative itself, already referred to, of the coming of the wise men, who sought Him with their gifts from a place afar off, and fell down and worshipped Him. Such too, is the account of His baptism, which forms the Second Lesson of the feast of the Epiphany, when the Holy Ghost descended on Him, and a Voice from heaven acknowledged Him to be the Son of God. And if we look at the Gospels read throughout the season, we shall find them all containing some kingly action of Christ, the Mediator between God and man.

Thus in the Gospel for the First Sunday, He manifests His glory in the temple at the age of twelve years, sitting among the doctors, and astonishing them with His wisdom. In the Gospel for the Second Sunday He manifests His glory at the wedding feast, when He turned the water into wine, a miracle not of necessity or urgency, but especially an august and bountiful act—the act of a King, who out of His abundance gave a gift to His own, therewith to make merry with their friends. In the Third Sunday, the leper worships Christ, who thereupon heals him; the centurion, again, reminds Him of His Angels and ministers, and He speaks the word, and his servant is restored forthwith. In the Fourth, a storm arises on the lake, while He is peacefully sleeping, without care or sorrow, on a pillow; then He rises and rebukes the winds and the sea, and a calm follows, deep as that of His own soul, and the beholders worship Him. And next He casts out Legion, after the man possessed with it had also "run and worshipped Him [2]." In the Fifth, we hear of His kingdom on earth, and of the enemy sowing tares amid the good seed. And in the Sixth, of His second Epiphany from heaven, "with power and great glory."

Such is the series of manifestations which the Sundays after the Epiphany bring before us. When He is with the doctors in the temple. He is manifested as a prophet—in turning the water into wine, as a priest—in His miracles of healing, as a bounteous Lord, giving out of His abundance—in His rebuking the sea, as a Sovereign, whose word is law—in the parable of the wheat and tares, as a guardian and ruler—in His second coming, as a lawgiver and judge.

And as in these Gospels we hear of our Savior's greatness, so in the Epistles and First Lessons we hear of the privileges and the duties of the new people, whom He has formed to show forth His praise. Christians are at once the temple of Christ, and His worshippers and ministers *in* the temple; they are the Bride of the Lamb taken collectively, and taken individually, they are the friends of the Bridegroom and the guests at the marriage feast. In these various points of view are they presented to us in the Services during these weeks. In the Lessons from the prophet Isaiah we read of the gifts and privileges, the characteristics, the power, the fortunes of the Church—how widely spreading, even throughout all the Gentiles; how awful and high, how miraculously endowed, how revered, how powerful upon earth, how rich in temporal goods, how holy, how pure in doctrine, how full of the Spirit. And in the Epistles for the successive Sundays, we hear of the duties and distinguishing marks of her true members, principally as laid down in the twelfth and thirteenth chapters of St. Paul to the Romans; then as the same Apostle enjoins them upon the Colossians; and then in St. John's exhortations in his General Epistle.

The Collects are of the same character, as befit the supplications of subjects coming before their King. The first is for knowledge and power, the second is for peace, the third is for strength in our infirmities, the fourth is for help in temptation, the fifth is for protection, and the sixth is for preparation and purification against Christ's second coming. There is none which would suit a season of trial, or of repentance, or of waiting, or of exultation—they befit a season of peace, thanksgiving, and adoration, when Christ is not manifested in pain, conflict, or victory, but in the tranquil possession of His kingdom. It will be sufficient to make one reflection, which suggests itself from what I have been saying.

You will observe, then, that the only display of royal greatness, the only season of majesty, homage, and glory, which our Lord had on earth, was in His infancy and youth. Gabriel's message to Mary was in its style and manner such as befitted an Angel speaking to Christ's Mother. Elisabeth, too, saluted Mary, and the future Baptist his hidden Lord, in the same honorable way. Angels announced His birth, and the shepherds worshipped. A star appeared, and the wise men rose from the East and made Him offerings. He was brought to the temple, and Simeon took Him in His arms, and returned thanks for Him. He grew to twelve years old, and again He appeared in the temple, and took His seat in the midst of the doctors. But here His earthly majesty had its end, or if seen afterwards, it was but now and then, by glimpses and by sudden gleams, but with no steady sustained light, and no diffused radiance. We are told at the close of the last-mentioned narrative, "And He went down with His parents, and came to Nazareth, *and was subjected, unto them* [3]." His subjection and servitude now began in fact. He had come in the form of a servant, and now He took on Him a servant's office. How much is contained in the idea of His subjection! And it began, and His time of glory ended, when He was twelve years old.

Solomon, the great type of the Prince of Peace, reigned forty years, and his name and greatness was known far and wide through the East. Joseph, the much-loved son of Jacob, who in an earlier age of the Church, was a type of Christ in His kingdom, was in power and favor eighty years, twice as long as Solomon. But Christ, the true Revealer of secrets, and the Dispenser of the bread of life, the true wisdom and majesty of the Father, manifested His glory but in His early years, and then the Sun of Righteousness was clouded. For He was not to reign really, till He left the world. He has reigned ever since; nay, reigned in the world, though He is not in sensible presence in it—the invisible King of a visible kingdom—for He came on earth but to show what His reign would be, after He had left it, and to submit to suffering and dishonor, that He *might* reign.

It often happens, that when persons are in serious illnesses, and in delirium in consequence, or other disturbance of mind, they have some few minutes of respite in the midst of it, when they are even more than themselves, as if to show us what they really are, and to interpret for us what else would be dreary.

And again, some have thought that the minds of children have on them traces of something more than earthly, which fade away as life goes on, but are the promise of what is intended for them hereafter. And somewhat in this way, if we may dare compare ourselves with our gracious Lord, in a parallel though higher way, Christ descends to the shadows of this world, with the transitory tokens on Him of that future glory into which He could not enter till He had suffered. The star burned brightly over Him for a while, though it then faded away.

We see the same law, as it may be called, of Divine Providence in other cases also. Consider, for instance, how the prospect of our Lord's passion opens upon the Apostles in the sacred history. Where did they hear of it? "Moses and Elias on the mountain appeared with Him in glory, and spake of His decease, which He should accomplish at Jerusalem [4]." That is, the season of His bitter trial was preceded by a short gleam of the glory which was to be, when He was suddenly transfigured, "and the fashion of His countenance was altered, and His raiment was white and glistering [5]." And with this glory in prospect, our Lord abhorred not to die: as it is written, "Who for the joy that was set before Him, endured the Cross, despising the shame."

Again, He forewarned His Apostles that they in like manner should be persecuted, for righteousness' sake, and be afflicted and delivered up, and hated and killed. Such was to be their life in this world, "that if in this world only they had had hope in Christ, they had been of all men most miserable [6]." Well then, observe, their trial too was preceded by a season of peace and pleasantness, in anticipation of their future reward; for before the day of Pentecost, for forty days Christ was with them, soothing, comforting, confirming them, "and speaking of the things pertaining unto the kingdom of God [7]." As Moses stood on the mount and saw the promised land and all its riches, and yet Joshua had to fight many battles before he got possession, so did the Apostles, before descending into the valley of the shadow of death, whence naught of heaven was to be seen, stand upon the heights, and look over that valley, which they had to cross, to the city of the living God beyond it.

And so again, St. Paul, after many years of toil, refers back to a time when he had a celestial vision, anticipatory of what was to be his blessedness in the end.

"I knew a man in Christ," he says, meaning himself, "about fourteen years ago, caught up to the third heaven . . . And I knew such a man . . . how that he was caught up into Paradise, and heard unspeakable words, which it is not lawful for a man to utter [8]." St. Paul then, as the twelve Apostles, and as our Lord before him, had his brief season of repose and consolation before the battle.

And lastly: the whole Church also may be said to have had a similar mercy vouchsafed to it at first, in anticipation of what is to be in the end. We know, alas, too well, that, according to our Lord's account of it, tares are to be with the wheat, fish of every kind in the net, all through its sojourning on earth. But in the end, "the saints shall stand before the throne of God, and serve Him day and night in His temple: and the Lamb shall feed them, and shall lead them unto living fountains of waters," and there shall be no more "sorrow nor pain, nor any thing that defileth or worketh abomination," "for without are dogs, and sorcerers, and whoremongers, and murderers, and idolaters, and whosoever loveth and maketh a lie." Now was not this future glory shadowed forth in that infancy of the Church, when before the seal of the new dispensation was opened and trial began, "there was silence in heaven for half an hour;" and "the disciples continued daily with one accord in the temple, and in prayers, breaking bread from house to house, being of one heart, and of one soul, eating their meat with gladness and singleness of heart, praising God, and having favor with all the people [9];" while hypocrites and "liars," like Ananias and Sapphira, were struck dead, and "sorcerers," like Simon, were detected and denounced?

To conclude; let us thankfully cherish all seasons of peace and joy which are vouchsafed us here below. Let us beware of abusing them, and of resting in them, of forgetting that they *are* special privileges, of neglecting to look out for trouble and trial, as our due and our portion. Trial is our portion here—we must not think it strange when trial comes after peace. Still God mercifully does grant a respite now and then; and perhaps He grants it to us the more, the more careful we are not to abuse it. For all seasons we must thank Him, for time of sorrow and time of joy, time of warfare and time of peace. And the more we thank Him for the one, the more we shall be drawn to thank Him for the other. Each has its own proper fruit, and its own peculiar blessedness. Yet our mortal flesh shrinks from the one, and of itself prefers the other;—it prefers rest to toil, peace to war, joy to sorrow, health to pain and sickness. When then Christ gives us what is pleasant, let us take it as refreshment by the way, that we may, when God calls, go in the strength of that meat forty days and forty nights unto

Horeb, the mount of God. Let us rejoice in Epiphany with trembling, that at Septuagesima we may go into the vineyard with the laborers with cheerfulness, and may sorrow in Lent with thankfulness; let us rejoice now, not as if we have attained, but in hope of attaining. Let us take our present happiness, not as our true rest, but, as what the land of Canaan was to the Israelites,—a type and shadow of it. If we now enjoy God's ordinances, let us not cease to pray that they may prepare us for His presence hereafter. If we enjoy the presence of friends, let them remind us of the communion of saints before His throne. Let us trust in nothing here, yet draw hope from every thing—that at length the Lord may be our everlasting light, and the days of our mourning may be ended.

[1] Hab. ii. 20.
[2] Mark v. 6.
[3] Luke ii. 51.
[4] Luke ix. 30, 31.
[5] Luke ix. 29.
[6] 1 Cor. xv. 19.
[7] Acts i. 3.
[8] 2 Cor. xii. 3, 4.
[9] Acts ii. 46, 47.

Reflection.

B. CATHOLIC

The first seven (beginning in 1848) of Newman's Catholic sermons show how entirely he threw himself into the "Catholic system." The old mastery is there, the style, the concrete illustrations, the psychological insight, the use of Holy Scripture, the stress on the moral preparation needed for receiving the truth; —it is authentic Newman, and entirely

Catholic. Newman could always enter into the minds of others, and so now the simplicity of these sermons is perhaps their most striking characteristic. His humility and docility, which were so remarked on at the time, showed itself even in the matter of delivery. As an Anglican he had always read his sermons. Now, anxious to avoid all singularity, he conformed to the Catholic custom. The last sermon of the seven, on our Lady, accounts very effectively for our Lord's apparent coldness towards her, especially His turning aside of the praise of the woman from the crowd (Luke xi, 27).

In the eighth sermon, the preaching of which took place in 1870, in his church at the Birmingham Oratory the parable of the unjust steward is given a moral application. One sentence in it, "not to do good is really to do evil," helps us to understand the cause of the great cross of Newman's life—that he was so often hindered from doing good, whether this was owing to the attitude of those in authority or to the slander of his opponents. He knew, and in view of the history of the Oxford Movement, he could not help knowing, that Almighty God had given him the greatest natural talents, and yet during so much of his Catholic life he found himself condemned to idleness, his sword rusting in its scabbard, through no fault of his.

The last sermon (in 1873) is taken up with grim forebodings about the spread and future course of infidelity, more terrible even than those he was to utter six years later, when he was made a Cardinal The future is foretold with a disturbing accuracy—the absence of all spiritual beliefs and the weakening of the non-Catholic religious bodies. In 2017 we have learned how prescient he was.

VIII. The Omnipotence of God the Reason for Faith and Hope
Fourth Sunday after Epiphany, January 30th, 1848.

Our Lord commanded the winds and the sea, and the men who saw it marveled saying, what manner of man is this, for the winds and the sea obey him? It was a miracle. It showed our

Lord's power over nature. And therefore they wondered, because they could not understand, and rightly, how any man could have power over nature, unless that power was given him by God.

Nature goes on her own way and we cannot alter it. Man cannot alter it, he can only use it. Matter, for instance, falls downward, earth, stone, iron all fall to the earth when left to themselves. Again, left to themselves, they cannot move *except* by falling. They never move except they are pulled or pushed forward. Water again never stands in a heap or a mass, but flows out on all sides as far as it can. Fire again always burns, or tends to burn. The wind blows to and fro, without any discoverable rule or law, and we cannot tell how it will blow tomorrow by seeing how it blows today. We see all these things. They have their own way; we cannot alter them.

All we attempt to do is to use them; we take them as we find them and we use them. We don't attempt to change the nature of fire, earth, air or water, but we observe what the nature of each is, and we try to turn it to account. We turn steam to account, and use it in carriages and ships; we turn fire to account and use it in a thousand ways. We use the things of nature, we submit to the laws of nature, and we avail ourselves of them; but we do not command nature. We do not attempt to alter it, but we merely direct it to our own purposes.

Far different was it with our Lord: He used indeed the winds and the water--(He used the water when He got into a boat, and used the wind when He suffered the sail to be spread over Him). He used, but more than this, He commanded, the winds and the waves—He had power to rebuke, to change, to undo the course of nature, as well as to make use of it. He was above nature. He had power over nature. This is what made the men marvel.

Experienced seamen can make use of the winds and the waves to get to the shore. Nay, even in a storm they know how to avail themselves of them, they have their rules what to do, and they are on the look out, taking advantage of everything that happens. But our Lord did not condescend to do this. He did not instruct them how to manage their sails, or how to steer the vessel, but He addressed Himself directly to winds and waves, and stopped them, making them do that which was against their nature.

So again, when Lazarus was ill, our Lord might have gone to him, and have recommended the fitting medicine, and the treatment, which would cure him. He did nothing of the kind— He let him die—so much so that St. Martha said when He at length came, "Lord, if Thou hadst been here, my brother had not died" (John 11). But our Lord had a reason. He wished to show His power over nature. He wished to triumph over death. So, instead of hindering Lazarus from dying by the art of medicine, He triumphed over death by a miracle.

No one has power over nature but He who made it. None can work a miracle but God. When miracles are wrought it is a proof that God is present. And therefore it is that, whenever God visits the earth, He works miracles. It is the claim He makes upon our attention. He thereby reminds us that He is the Creator. He who did, alone can undo. He who made, alone can destroy. He who gave nature its laws, alone can change those laws. He who made fire to burn, food to nourish, water to flow, iron to sink, He alone can make fire harmless, food needless, water firm and solid, iron light, and therefore whether He sent forth the Prophets or the Apostles, Moses, Joshua, Samuel, or Elias, He always sent them with miracles, to show His presence with His servants. Then all things began to change their nature; the Egyptians were tormented with strange plagues, the waters stood in a heap for the Chosen people to pass over, they were fed with manna in the desert, the sun and the moon stood still—because God was there.

This then was what made the men marvel, when our Lord stilled the storm upon the sea. It was a proof to them that God was there, though they saw Him not. Nay, God was there and they saw Him—for Christ was God—but whether they learned this high and sacred truth or not from the miracle, so far they understood that God really was there. His hand was there, His power was there, and therefore they feared.

You have read in books, I dare say, stories of great men who come in disguise, and at length are known by their voice, or by some deed, which betrays them. Their voices, or their words, or their manner, or their exploit, is their token—it is a sort of handwriting. And so when God walks the earth, He gives us means of knowing that He does so, though He is a hidden God, and does not display His glory openly. Power over nature is the token He gives us that He, the Creator of Nature, is in the midst of us.

And therefore God is called almighty—this is His distinguishing attribute. Man is powerful only by means of nature. He uses nature as his instrument, but God has no need of nature, in order to accomplish His will, but works His great work, sometimes by means of nature, and sometimes without nature, as it please Him.

And you will observe this attribute of God is the only one mentioned in the Creed. "I believe in God, the Father almighty." It is not said "I believe in God the Father All merciful, or All holy, or All wise," though all these attributes are His also, but "I believe in God the Father *Almighty*." Why is this? It is plain why —because this attribute is the reason *why* we *believe*. Faith is the beginning of religion, and therefore the almightiness of God is made the beginning and first of His attributes, and just the attribute which ought to be mentioned in the Creed. We should not be able to believe in Him, did we not know that He is almighty. Nothing is too hard to believe of Him to whom nothing is too hard to do. You may recollect that when it was prophesied to Abraham that the old Sarah his wife should have a son, Sarah laughed. Why did she laugh? Because she did not bear sufficiently in mind that God is almighty. Therefore the Lord said to her, "Is anything *hard* for God?" (Gen. 18). And in like manner our Lord in the Gospel of this day, when He commanded the winds and the sea, said "Why are ye fearful, O ye of little *faith*?" If they had had a firm perception of His almightiness, they would have been sure that He could bring them out of danger. But when they saw Him asleep in the boat, they could not believe that they were safe, not understanding that He, awake or asleep, was almighty.

This thought is very important to us at this day, because it will be a means of sustaining our faith. Why do you believe all the strange and marvelous acts recorded in Scripture? Because God is almighty and can do them. Why do you believe that a Virgin conceived and bore a Son? Because it is God's act, and He can do anything. As the Angel Gabriel said to the Blessed Virgin, "No word is impossible with God." On the other hand, when holy Zacharias was told by the Angel that the old Elizabeth, his wife, should conceive, he said, "Whence shall I know this?" and he was punished at once for disbelieving. Why do you believe that our Lord rose from the dead? Why, that He redeemed us all with His precious blood? Why, that He washes away our sins in Baptism? Why do you believe in the power and grace, which attends the other sacraments? Why do you believe in the resurrection of our bodies? You believe it because nothing is too hard for God—because however wonderful a thing may be, He can do it. Why do you believe in the virtue of holy relics? Why do you believe that the Saints hear your prayers? Because nothing is too hard for the Lord.

This especially applies to the great miracle of the Altar. Why do you believe that the Priest changes the bread into the body of Christ? Because God is almighty and nothing is too hard for Him. And moreover you know, as I have said, that miracles are the signs and tokens of God's presence. If then He is present in the Catholic Church, it is *natural* to expect that He will work some miracles, and if He did no miracle, we might be almost tempted to believe that He had left His Church.

When you assist at the holy sacrifice of the Altar and bow down at the elevation, and whenever you make an act of faith in God, steadily contemplating all that He has done for us in the Gospel, recollect God is almighty, and it will enable you to be bolder and more determined in making it. Say, I believe this and that, because God is almighty—I do not worship a creature: I am not the servant of a God of restricted power. But since God can *do* everything, I can *believe* everything. There is nothing too much for Him to do, and nothing too hard for me to believe. I will enlarge my heart. I will go forward in a generous way. "Open thy mouth wide," says God to me, "and I will fill it." Well, I do open my mouth, I desire to be fed with His words. I desire to live and to thrive by every word, which He speaks. I desire to say with the prophet, "Speak, Lord, for thy servant heareth." I will not grudge, I will not doubt, because I believe that which takes away all doubting. All acts of divine power do but fall under, and are but instances of, that universal attribute on which I believe, omnipotence. If God can do all things, He can do this. He can do much more than this. Wonderful as this or that may be to our narrow minds, still if we knew all, we should see that this, whatever it is, was but one thing out of many. This is what our Lord signified to holy Nathanael. Nathanael, struck with something that our Lord said, cried out, "Rabbi, Thou art the Son of God, Thou art the King of Israel." He made answer "Believest thou on this account? Thou shalt see a greater thing than this." There is no end of God's power; it is inexhaustible. Let there be no end to our faith. Let us not be startled at what we are called on to believe; let us still be on the look out. Some people are slow to believe the miracles ascribed to the Saints. Now we know that such miracles are not part of the *faith*; they have no place in the Creed. And some are reported on better evidence than others. Some may be true, and others not so certainly true. Others again may be true but not miracles. But still why should they be *surprised* to hear of miracles? Are they beyond the power of God, and is not God present with the Saints, and has He not wrought miracles of old? Are miracles a new thing? There is no reason to be surprised, on the contrary; because in the Sacrifice of the Mass He works daily the most wonderful of miracles at the word of the priest. If then He does daily a miracle greater than any that can be named, why should we be surprised to hear reports of His doing other and lesser miracles now and then?

The Gospel of the day then sets before us the duty of *faith*, and rests it upon God's almightiness or omnipotence, as it is called. Nothing is too hard for Him, and we believe what the Church tells us of His deeds and providences, because He can do whatsoever He will. But there is another grace, which the Gospel teaches us, and that is *hope* or *trust*. You observe that when the storm came, the disciples were in great *distress*. They thought some great calamity was coming on them. Therefore Christ said to them, "Why are ye *fearful*?" Hope and fear are contrary to each other; they feared because they did not hope. To hope is, not only to believe in God, but to believe and be certain that He loves us and means well to us; and therefore it is a great Christian grace.

For faith without hope is not certain to bring us to Christ. The devils believe and tremble (James 2). They believe, but they do not come to Christ—because they do not hope, but despair. They despair of getting any good from Him. Rather they know that they shall get nothing but evil, so they keep away. You recollect the man possessed of the devil said: "What have we to do with Thee, Jesus the Son of God—art Thou come hither to torment us before the time?" (Matt. 8). The coming of Christ was no comfort to them, the contrary: they shrank from Him. They knew He meant them not good, but punishment. But to men He meant good, and it is by knowing and feeling this that men are brought to Him. They will not come to God till they are sure of this. They must believe that He is not only almighty, but all merciful also.

Faith is founded on the knowledge that God is almighty, hope is founded on the knowledge that God is all merciful. And the presence of our Lord and Savior Jesus Christ excites us to hope quite as much as to faith, because His very name Jesus means Savior, and because He was so loving, meek, and bountiful when He was on earth.

He said to the disciples when the storm arose, "Why are ye *fearful*?" That is, you ought to hope, you ought to trust, you ought to repose your heart on Me. I am not only almighty, but I am all merciful. I have come on earth because I am most loving to you. Why am I here, why am I in human flesh, why have I these hands which I stretch out to you, why have I these eyes from which the tears of pity flow, except that I wish you well, that I wish to save you? The storm cannot hurt you if *I* am with you. Can you be better placed than under my protection? Do you doubt My power or My will, do you think Me *negligent* of you that I sleep in the ship, and *unable* to help you except I am awake? Wherefore do you doubt? Wherefore do you fear? Have I been so long with you, and you do not yet trust Me, and cannot remain in peace and quiet by My side?"

And so, my Brethren, He says to us now. All of us who live in this mortal life, have our troubles. You have your troubles, but when you are in trouble, and the waves seem to mount high, and to be soon to overwhelm you, make an act of faith, an act of hope, in your God and Savior. He calls you to Him who has His mouth and His hands full of blessings for you. He says: "Come unto Me, all that labor and are laden, and I will refresh you" (Matt. 11). "All ye that thirst," He cries out by His prophet, "come ye to the waters, and ye that have no money, haste ye, buy, and eat."

Never let the thought come into your mind that God is a hard master, a severe master. It is true the day will come when He will come as a just Judge, but now is the time of mercy. Improve it and make the most of the time of grace. "Behold now is the acceptable time, behold now is the day of salvation." This is the day of hope, this is the day of work, this is the day of activity. "The night cometh when no man can work," but we are children of the light and of the day, and therefore despondency, coldness of heart, fear, sluggishness are sins in us. Temptations indeed come on you to murmur, but resist them, drive them aside, pray God to help you with His mighty grace. He allows no temptation to befall us, which He does not give us grace to surmount. Do not let your hope give way, but "lift up the languid hands and the relaxed knees" (Heb. 12). "Lose not your confidence, which hath a great reward" (Heb. 10). Seek His face who ever dwells in real and bodily presence in His Church. Do at least as much as what the disciples did. They had but little faith, they feared, they had not any great confidence and peace, but at least they did not keep away from Christ. They did not sit still sullenly, but they came to Him. Alas, our very best state is not higher than the Apostles' worst state. Our Lord blamed them as having *little* faith, because they cried out to Him. I wish we Christians of this day did as much as this. I wish we went as far as to cry out to Him in alarm. I wish we had only as much faith and hope as that which Christ thought so little in His first disciples. At least imitate the apostles in their weakness, if you can't imitate them in their strength.

If you can't act as saints, at least act as Christians. Do not keep from Him, but, when you are in trouble, come to Him day by day asking Him earnestly and perseveringly for those favors, which He alone can give. And as He on this occasion spoken of in the Gospel, blamed indeed the disciples, but did for them what they asked, so, (we will trust in His great mercy), though He discerns much infirmity in you which ought not to be there, yet He will deign to rebuke the winds and the sea, and say "Peace, be still," and there will be a great calm.

May this be your happy lot, my dear Brethren, and may the blessing of God Almighty, the Father, etc.

Reflection.

IX. Preparation for the Judgment
Septuagesima. February 20th, 1848

The last shall be first and the first last, for many are called, but few are chosen. Such are the words with which the Gospel of this day ends, which is the Parable of the Laborers in the Vineyard. In that parable, you know well, my Brethren, the Master of the Vineyard calls into his Vineyard all the laborers he can get together. He calls them in at different times, some in the morning, some at noon, some shortly before the evening. When the evening is come, he bids his paymaster call them together and give them their wages for the day past. It is very plain what this means. The Master of the Vineyard is our Lord and Savior. We are the laborers. The evening is the hour of death, when we shall each receive the reward of our labor, if we have labored well.

There is more in the parable than this, but I shall not go into the details of it. I shall here content myself with the general sketch I have taken of it, and with the words with which it concludes, "The last shall be first and the first last, for," etc.

Well is the hour of death described as the evening. There is something in the evening especially calm and solemn, fitly representing the hour of death. How peculiar, how unlike anything else, is a summer evening, when after the fever and heat of the day, after walking, or after working, after any toil, we cease from it, and for a few minutes enjoy the grateful feeling of rest! Especially is it so in the country, where evening tends to fill us with peace and tranquility. The decreasing light, the hushing of all sounds, the sweet smell, perhaps, of the woods or the herbs which are all about us, the mere act of resting, and the consciousness that night is coming, all tend to tranquillize us and make us serious. Alas, I know that in persons of irreligious mind it has a very different effect, and while other men are raised to the love of God and Christ and the thought of heaven by the calm evening, *they* are but led to the thought of evil and deeds of sin. But I am speaking of those who live towards God and train their hearts heavenward, and I say that such persons find in the calm evening but an incitement to greater devotion, greater renunciation of the world. It does but bring before them the coming down of death, and leads them with the Apostle to die daily. Evening is the time for divine visitations. The Lord God visited Adam after he had sinned in the garden, in the cool of the evening. In the evening the patriarch Isaac went out to meditate in the field. In the evening our Lord discovered Himself to the two disciples who went to Emmaus. In the same evening He appeared to the Eleven, breathed on them, gave them the Holy Ghost, and invested them with the power of remitting and retaining sins. Nay even in a town the evening is a soothing time. It is soothing to be at the end of the week, having completed the week's work, with the day of rest before us. It is soothing, even after the day of rest, though labor is in store for us against the morrow, to find ourselves in the evening of the day. It is a feeling that almost all must be able to bear witness to, as something peculiar, as something fitly prefiguring that awful time when our work will be done, and we shall rest from our labors.

That indeed will be emphatically our evening, when the long day of life is over and eternity is at hand. Man goeth forth to his work and to his labor until the evening, and then the night cometh when no man can work. There is something inexpressibly solemn and subduing in that time, when work is done and judgment is coming. O my brethren, we must each of us in his turn, sooner or later, arrive at that hour. Each of us must come to the evening of life. Each of us must enter on eternity. Each of us must come to that quiet, awful time, when we appear before the Lord of the Vineyard, and answer for the deeds done in the body, whether they be good or bad. That, my dear Brethren, you will have to undergo. Every one of you must undergo the Particular Judgment, and it will be the stillest, awfullest time, which you ever can experience. It will be the dread moment of expectation, when your fate for eternity is in the balance, and when you are about to be sent forth the companion of saints or devils without possibility of change. There can be no change, there can be no reversal. As that judgment decides it, so it will be for ever and ever. Such is the particular judgment. The general judgment at the end of the world will be a time of dreadful publicity, and will be full of the terrible brightness of the Judge. The trumpet of the Archangel will sound, and the Lord will descend from heaven in lightning. The graves will open. The sun and the moon will be darkened and this earth will pass away. This is not the time of evening, but rather it will be a tempest in the midst of the night.

But the parable in the Gospel speaks of the time of evening, and by the evening is meant, not the end of the world, but the time of death. And really perhaps it will be as awful, though very different, that solitary judgment, when the soul stands before its Maker, to answer for itself. O who can tell which judgment is the more terrible, the silent secret judgment, or the open glorious coming of the Judge. It will be most terrible certainly, and it comes first, to find ourselves by ourselves, one by one, in His presence, and to have brought before us most vividly all the thoughts, words and deeds of this past life. Who will be able to bear the sight of himself?

And yet we shall be obliged steadily to confront ourselves and to see ourselves. In this life we shrink from knowing our real selves. We do not like to know how sinful we are. We love those who prophesy smooth things to us, and we are angry with those who tell us of our faults. But then, not one fault only, but all the secret, as well as evident, defects of our character will be clearly brought out. We shall see what we feared to see here, and much more. And then, when the full sight of ourselves comes to us, who will not wish that he had known more of himself here, rather than leaving it for the inevitable day to reveal it all to him!

I am speaking, not only of the bad, but of the good. Those indeed who have died in neglect of good, it will be a most insufferably dreadful sight to them, and they will not have long to contemplate it, in silence, for they will be hurried away to their punishment. But I speak of holy souls, souls that will be saved, and I say that to these the sight of themselves will be intolerable, and it will be a torment to them to see what they really are and the sins, which lie against them. And hence some writers have said that their horror will be such that of their own will, and from a holy indignation against themselves, they will be ready to plunge into Purgatory in order to satisfy divine justice, and to be clear of what is to their own clear sense and spiritual judgment so abominable.

We do not know how great an evil sin is. We do not know how subtle and penetrating an evil it is. It circles round us and enters in every seam, or rather at every pore. It is like dust covering everything, defiling every part of us, and requiring constant attention, constant cleansing. Our very duties cover us with this miserable dust and dirt. As we labor in God's vineyard and do His will, the while from the infirmity of our nature we sin in lesser matters even when we do good in greater, so that when the evening comes, with all our care, in spite of the sacraments of the Church, in spite of our prayers and our penance, we are covered with the heat and defilement of the day.

This, I say, will be the case even with religious persons who have labored to save their souls; but Oh! how miserable will be the case of those who have never had religious thoughts! There are persons, for instance, who cannot bear thought of any kind, who cannot bear an hour's silent reflection. It would be a great punishment to many a man to be obliged to think of himself.

Many men like to live in a whirl, in some excitement or other which keeps their minds employed, and keeps them from thinking of themselves. How many a man, e.g. employs all his leisure time in learning merely the news of the day. He likes to read the periodical publications, he likes to know what is going on in the four quarters of the earth. He fills his mind with matters which either do not concern him, or concern only his temporal welfare; with what they are doing in various parts of England, what Parliament is doing, what is done in Ireland, what is done on the Continent; nay he descends to little matters of no importance, rather than entertain that thought which must come on him, if not before, at least in the evening of life and when he stands before his Judge. Others are full of projects for making money; be they high or be they low, that is their pursuit, they covet wealth and they live in the thought how they may get it. They are alive to inventions and improvements in their particular trade, and to nothing else. They rival each other. They as it were, run a race with each other, not a heavenly race, such as the Apostle's who ran for a crown incorruptible, but a low earthly race, each trying by all means in his power to distance his neighbor in what is called the favor of the public, making this their one end, and thinking nothing at all of religion. And others take up some doctrine whether of politics or of trade or of philosophy, and spend their lives upon it; they go about to recommend it in every way they can. They speak, they write, they labor for an object which will perish with this world, which cannot pass with them through the grave. The holy Apostle says "Blessed are they that die in the Lord, for their works do *follow them*" (Apoc. 14). Good works follow us, bad works follow us, but everything else is worth nothing; everything else is but chaff. The whirl and dance of worldly matters is but like the whirling of chaff or dust, nothing comes of it; it lasts through the day, but it is not to be found in the evening. And yet how many immortal souls spend their lives in nothing better than making themselves giddy with this whirl of politics, of party, or religious opinion, or money getting, of which nothing can ever come.

Observe in the parable the Master of the Vineyard did but one thing. He told his servant to "call the laborers and give them their hire." He did but ask *what they had done*. He did not ask what their opinion was about science, or about art, or about the means of wealth, or about public affairs; he did not ask them if they knew the nature of the vine for which they had been laboring. They were not required to know how many kinds of vines there were in the world, and what countries vines could grow in, and where they could not. They were not called upon to give their opinion what soils were best for the vines. They were not examined in the minerals, or the shrubs, or in anything else, which was found in the vineyard, but this was the sole question, whether they had *worked* in the vineyard.

First they must be in the vineyard, then they must work in it; these were the two things. So will it be with us after death. When we come into God's presence, we shall be asked two things, whether we were in the Church, and whether we worked in the Church. Everything else is worthless. Whether we have been rich or poor, whether we have been learned or unlearned, whether we have been prosperous or afflicted, whether we have been sick or well, whether we have had a good name or a bad one, all this will be far from the work of that day. The single question will be, are we Catholics and are we good Catholics? If we have not been, it will avail nothing that we have been ever so honored here, ever so successful, have had ever so good a name. And if we have been, it will matter nothing though we have been ever so despised, ever so poor, ever so hardly pressed, ever so troubled, ever so unfriended. Christ will make up everything to us, if we have been faithful to Him; and He will take everything away from us, if we have lived to the world.

Then will be fulfilled the awful words of the parable. Many that are last shall be first, for many are called but few are chosen.

Then, also, will it be seen how many have received grace and have not profited by it. Then will be seen how many were called, called by the influence of God's grace, called into the Church, yet how few have a place prepared in Heaven. Then will be seen how many resisted their conscience, resisted the call of Christ to follow Him, and so are lost. This is the day both of divine grace and of patience. God gives grace and is patient with us, but when death comes, there is no more time either for grace or for patience. Grace is exhausted, patience is exhausted. Nothing remains but judgment, a terrible judgment on those who have lived in disobedience.

And oh! what a sight it will be, what an unexpected sight, at the last day and public judgment to be present at that revelation of all hearts! How different persons will then seem, from what they seem now! How will the last be first, and the first last! Then those whom the world looked up to, will be brought low, and those who were little esteemed, will be exalted. Then will it be found who are the real movers in the world's affairs, those who sustained the cause of the Church or who influenced the fortunes of empires, were not the great and powerful, not those whose names are known in the world, but the humble despised followers of the Lamb, the meek saint, the man full of prayer and good works whom the world passed by; the hidden band of saintly witnesses, whose voice day by day ascended to Christ; the sufferers who seemed to be living for nothing; the poor whom the proud world thought but an offence and a nuisance. When that Day comes, may it reveal good for each of you, my Brethren, and may the blessing, etc.

Reflection.

X. The Calls of Grace
Sexagesima, February 27th, 1848

In the parable of the Sower, which has formed the Gospel for
this day, we have set before us four descriptions of men, all of
whom receive the word of God. The sower sows first on the
hard ground or road, then on the shallow earth or rock, then on
a ground where other seeds were sown, and lastly on really
good, rich, well-prepared soil. By the sower is meant the
preacher; and by the seed the word preached; and by the rock,
the road, the preoccupied ground, and the good soil, are meant
four different states of mind of those who hear the word. Now
here we have a picture laid out before us, which will, through
God's mercy, provide us with a fitting subject of thought this
evening.

First, let us consider the case of the hard ground and the seed
that was sown there—"some fell by the road and was trodden
down and the birds of the heaven ate it up." Such is the power
of the divine word, spoken by its appointed preacher; so
blessed and prospered is it by divine grace that it goes forth
like a dart or an arrow. Amos the prophet says: "Their arrows
are very sharp, in the heart of the King's enemies"; and
another prophet says: "I have hewn them by the prophet. I
have slain them with the words of My mouth." And so in the
book of the Apocalypse we read of our Lord as represented
with a sharp sword out of his mouth; and St. Paul speaks of the
sword of the Spirit, which is the Word of God. The word goeth
forth, as the prophet Isaias says, and does not return unto Him
void, but prospers in the thing whereto He sends it.

Nothing can stop it, but a closed heart. Nothing can resist it,
but a deliberately worldly, carnal and godless will—and such a
will can. But where the heart is ever so little softened, the
divine word enters it; where it is not softened, it lies on the
surface. It lies on the surface and we learn from the parable
the immediate consequence: "the birds of the air stole it away."
It did not lie there long. There was but the alternative—it was
admitted within, or the wind or the birds or the foot of the
passer-by, as it might be, destroyed it.

Now I can fancy some of those who hear me thinking that this is an extreme case—when perhaps it is their own. When they read or hear this picture of the seed falling on the hard wayside, they may hear it in an unconcerned way, as if they had not interest in it, when they may have a great concern in the description. There are a very great many persons whose hearts are like the hard wayside. Now I will explain what I mean. I suppose it occurs to all of us to hear names of persons mentioned, or to hear of events, or occurrences, which we hear one moment and forget the next: they simply pass through our minds and make no impression. Why? Because we never heard of them before; we take no interest in them, and so they don't take hold of us. They are like an unknown language, and go as they came.

But now supposing the person mentioned is one whose history we know. Supposing it is a public man, whom we have heard about or read of for years—Why, did we hear of anything happening to him, did we hear he had left the country, or fallen into misfortune, or fallen ill, or been promoted, or had died, his name kindles up a whole history, and we take great interest in the news brought us. We connect what we now hear with what we already know. And so you often may find, coming into a party of men, and saying this or that of a certain person, that the news produces a great effect on one, and is simply unmeaning to another. The latter turns off to some other subject at once, and is not struck, but the former expresses surprise, or pleasure or grief, and says: "Is it possible?" "I remember such a man twenty years ago—how he is changed, or how great a rise, or what a sad end." We might hear, as just now, that the king of the French has abdicated. One man says "I recollect his coming to the throne," and he will muse on it. To another the news is so many idle words, and he thinks nothing of it.

And much more—if the news concerned some dear friend, or some near relation. Did we hear even his name mentioned in conversation, our ears are so sharp that we should catch it at once; because the image of a person whom we know well is associated in our minds with a thousand thoughts—he has a place in us—he is, as it were, part of us. He has a long history written within us; his name has a deep meaning.

But you see the difference between one whose heart is hard, and one whose heart is softened. One man has often thought about religion, another never. The latter will be interested enough if you speak to him of things connected with this world, if you talk only of how to raise crops or how to make money in any way, or of any worldly amusement or pleasure, his attention is arrested at once. But if you speak to him about the four last things, about heaven or hell, death or judgment, he stares or laughs out. If you speak good and holy words to him, he hears and forgets. This is the dreadful case with many at death; religious persons say what they can to touch the dying man and the poor patient hears indeed, but hears without emotion, without thought of any kind. The words fall off, and have no effect—and so he dies. On the contrary some sacred place or sacred name is like a magic spell to those whose hearts are accustomed to the thought of religion, or are in any way disposed and prepared by God's grace. Take a person who has been tried by misfortune, or who has suffered the loss of some dear relative, or who has fallen into sin and is under compunctions, then when he hears the words "What shall I do to be saved?" or "After death, the judgment," or "believe and be saved," or "Comfort ye, comfort ye, my people," or "Christ died for sinners,"—such few words fit into his habitual state of mind, and at once kindle him—he cannot help listening—he seizes the word and devours it.

Nay we know that to holy people the very name of Jesus is a name to feed upon, a name to transport; or the name of Mary, or of both—"Jesu Mariae" and "Alma Redemptoris Mater"— Saints have gone into ecstasy upon the name. The picture, which it brings before the mind of Mother and Son, the Eternal Son and His high-favored Mother, awful transporting relationship, most human yet most divine, these are the words which can raise the dead and transfigure and beatify the living.

You will observe that, in the parable, not only did the fowls carry off the word of life, but the foot of the passer-by trampled it. I have hitherto spoken of those who were ignorant, careless and heartless, and from whom the devil stole the divine treasure, while they let it lie on the surface of their minds.

But there are others who are worse than this; who, as it were, trample on the divine words. Such are those who feel a disdain and hatred of the truth. It is an awful thing to say, but we see it before our eyes how many people there are who hate the doctrine, which Christ revealed and the Church teaches. Of course many do so in mere ignorance, and would feel and act otherwise, if they had the opportunity. But there are those, and not a few, who scorn and are irritated at the preaching of the word of life, and spurn it from them. It has been so from the beginning. Cain slew Abel; Joseph was stripped and sold by his brethren; David was hated by Saul; and above all our Lord was spat upon and put to death by the Jews. "He came unto His own and His own received Him not." And as He was abominated and cast out by a sinful generation, so, since He has departed, His word is abominated by the world still. Sometimes it is for want of love. You hear people revile the Church, ridicule the most sacred things, get angry directly they are mentioned, frown and change countenance, nay shake all over when they see a priest, suspect everything that is shocking and detestable as the characteristic of monk or nun, and spread from a deep prejudice the most untrue stories.

Sometimes from want of faith; they think it quite wonderful, beyond expression strange and marvelous, that men can be found to believe this or that doctrine; they won't believe they can; they think they pretend to believe what they don't; they look upon all educated Catholics as hypocrites—and sometimes it arises from a bad conscience and impatience at being told their duty. Our Lord bids us not cast our pearls before swine, but they trample them under their feet. This is what carnal, sensual people do. They wish to live their own way; they do not like to be warned of hell and judgment, and when the warning voice comes to them, they rise up against it, and think it a personal offence to themselves that it declares the truth of God. They put their foot upon it, and tread out the heavenly flame.

But I will now go on to mention a third case of hardness of heart, which not infrequently occurs, and that is, the case of those who get familiar with the word of life and then are not moved by it. When persons who are living in sin hear for the first time the sound of Catholic truth, they are affected by it; it is something new and the novelty of the doctrine is God's instrument. It is blest by God, to make an effect upon them. It moves and draws them. And then the worship of the Catholic Church is so overcoming—the holy forms, the sacred actions, the awful functions (Benediction, for instance), subdue them. They, as it were, give up, they surrender themselves to God, they feel themselves in the hands of their Savior. They are led to cry out: "Take me, make what Thou wilt of me." This lasts for some time, and in a number of cases, praised be God, it ends happily; this excitement and transport of mind leads on to a lasting conversion.

But in other cases it does not. A person is moved for a while, and then the excitement goes off. I have seen cases of this kind—many people may know them.

A man is on the point of making a real conversion; he is on the point of taking up religion seriously. He is on the point of putting one and one object alone before him as the end of his being and the aim of his life, to please God and save his soul. But all of a sudden a change comes over him. Almost while we turn our head and look another way, it has taken place. We look back to him and he is quite another man—or rather he is the same, the same as he was. He has lapsed into his old forgetfulness of religion, and when he has once relaxed, it is impossible to move him. There he is for ever.

And so, when a person is not exactly forgetful of religion, but has a form of religion; lives by rule and is called, and in a certain way is, a religious man; but is at one time moved to embrace that one true form of godliness which comes from heaven, putting aside his idols and vanities; *if* he neglects to take the step, *if* his courage fails him, or his pride stops him, or love of the world draws him back, and he gives up the notion, he is not what he was before. No, for he is worse. The latter state of that man is worse than the first. He was hard before, and now is he ten times as hard. Not only the good seed has been trampled on, but his heart has been trodden down; it is as hard as the pavement, and nothing will move him again.

This, alas, is often the case in places where truth has been preached for many years, compared with new places. In the new place you find the word prospers; but there is coldness, deadness, languor, tepidity, backwardness, insincerity, in the old.

There is a case of this hardness of heart still more awful. I have known the case of a person taking up religion for a time and seeming to be religious and then casting it off, and giving up even the belief in God, just like a brute of the field; and confessing it, confessing it in language such as this: —"I was religious once. Religion had its day with me. It grew up, like the grass, and it has come to nought like the grass. I can't revive it. It was a certain state of mind of a certain period of my life, but I have outgrown it."

And now, my dear Brethren, what other lesson can I draw from these considerations, than that which the Prophet gives us in the Psalm, and which the Apostle borrows from him: "Today if ye shall hear His voice, harden not your hearts, as in the provocation, according to the day of temptation in the wilderness ... Exhort one another every day whilst it is called today, lest any be hardened by the deceitfulness of sin" (Heb. 3, 13). 'When the heart is hard, the birds take away the divine seed. They do not bring it back; it goes for ever. Make the most of the precious time. Delay not—many a soul has been damned by delay. God's opportunities do not wait; they come and they go. The word of life waits not—if it is not appropriated by you, the devil will appropriate. He delays not, but has his eyes wide always and is ready to pounce down and carry off the gift, which you delay to use.

And if you are conscious that your hearts are hard, and are desirous that they should be softened, do not despair. All things are possible to you, through God's grace. Come to Him for the will and the power to do that to which He calls you. He never forsakes anyone who calls upon him. He never puts any trial on a man but He gives Him grace to overcome it. Do not despair then; nay do not despond, even though you do come to Him, yet are not at once exalted to overcome yourselves. He gives grace by little and little. It is by coming daily into His presence, that by degrees we find ourselves awed by that presence and able to believe and obey Him. Therefore if any one desires illumination to know God's will as well as strength to do it, let him come to Mass daily, if he possibly can. At least let him present himself daily before the Blessed Sacrament, and, as it were, offer his heart to His Incarnate Savior, presenting it as a reasonable offering to be influenced, changed and sanctified under the eye and by the grace of the Eternal Son.

And let him every now and then through the day make some short prayer or ejaculation, to the Lord and Savior, and again to His Blessed Mother, the immaculate most Blessed Virgin Mary, or again to his guardian Angel, or to his Patron Saint. Let him now and then collect his mind and place himself, as if in heaven, in the presence of God; as if before God's throne; let him fancy he sees the All-Holy Lamb of God, which taketh away the sin of the world. These are the means by which, with God's grace, he will be able in course of time to soften his heart—not all at once, but by degrees; not by his own power or wisdom, but by the grace of God blessing his endeavor.

Thus it is that Saints have begun. They have begun by these little things, and so become at length Saints. They were not saints all at once, but by little and little. And so we, who are not saints, must still proceed by the same road; by lowliness, patience, trust in God, recollection that we are in His presence, and thankfulness for His mercies.

And now, my Brethren, though I have said but a little on a large subject, I have said enough, not enough for the subject, but enough for you, enough for you to get a lesson from. May you lay it to heart, as I am sure you do and will, may you gain a blessing from it; and in this as in all things may the blessing of God Almighty, the Father, etc.

Reflection.

XI. Prejudice and Faith
Quinquagesima, March 5th, 1848

We have in the Gospel for this day what, I suppose, has raised the wonder of most readers of the New Testament. I mean the slowness of the disciples to take in the notion that our Lord was to suffer on the Cross. It can only be accounted for by the circumstance that a contrary opinion had strong possession of their minds—what we call a strong prejudice against the truth, in their cases an honest religious prejudice, the prejudice of honest religious minds, but still a deep and violent prejudice. When our Lord first declared it, St. Peter said, "Be it far from thee, Lord, this shall not happen to Thee." He spoke so strongly that the holy Evangelist says that he "took our Lord and began to rebuke Him." He did it out of reverence and love, as the occasion of it shows, but still that he spoke with warmth, with vehemence, is evident from the expression. Think then how deep his prejudice must have been.

This same prejudice accounts for what we find in today's gospel. Our Lord said, "Behold we go to Jerusalem, and all that is written of the Son of man shall be accomplished. For He shall be delivered to the Gentiles, and shall be mocked and scourged and spat upon; and after they have scourged Him, they will put Him to death, and the third day He shall rise again." Could words be plainer? Yet what effect had they on the disciples? "They understood none of these things, and this was hid from them, and they understood not the things that were said." Why hid? Because they had not eyes to see.

And so again after the resurrection, when they found the sepulcher empty, it is said, "They knew not the Scripture, that He must rise again from the dead." And when St. Mary Magdalene and the other women told them, "their words seemed to them as an idle tale, and they did not believe them"; and accordingly when our Lord appeared to them, "He upbraided them with their incredulity and hardness of heart, because they did not believe them who had seen Him after He was risen again."

This is certainly a very remarkable state of mind, and the record of it in the Gospels may serve to explain much which goes on among us, and to put us on our guard against ourselves, and to suggest to us the question, Are we in any respect in the same state of imperfection as these holy, but at that time prejudiced, disciples of our Lord and Savior?

It will be well to observe what the cause of their blindness was—it was a false interpretation which they had given to the Old Testament Scriptures, an interpretation which was common in their day, and which they had been taught by the Scribes and Pharisees, who sat in Moses' seat and pretended to teach them Moses' doctrine. It was the opinion of numbers at that day that the promised Messiah or Christ, who was coming, would be a great temporal Prince, like Solomon, only greater; that he was to have an earthly court, earthly wealth, earthly palaces, lands and armies and servants and the glory of a temporal kingdom. This was their idea—they looked for a deliverer, but thought he would come like Gideon, David, or Judas Maccabaeus, with sword and spear and loud trumpet, inflicting wounds and shedding blood, and throwing his captives into dungeons.

And they fancied Scripture taught this doctrine. They took parts of Scripture, which pleased their fancy, in the first place, and utterly put out of their minds such as went contrary to these. It is quite certain that the Prophet Isaias and other prophets speak of our Lord, then to come, as a conqueror. He speaks of Him as red with the blood of His enemies, and smiting in wrath the heads of diverse countries; as ruling kings with a rod of iron, and extending His dominion to the ends of the earth. It is also true that Scripture elsewhere speaks of the

Messias otherwise. He is spoken of as rejected of men, as a leper, as an outcast, as persecuted, as spat upon and pierced and slain. But these passages they put away from them. They did not let them produce their legitimate effects upon their hearts. They heard them with the ear and not with the head, and so it was all one as if they had not been written; to them they were not written. It did not occur to them that they possibly could mean, what nevertheless they did mean.

Therefore, when our Lord told them that He, He the Christ, was to be scourged and spat upon, they were taken by surprise, and they cried out, "Be it far from Thee, Lord—impossible, that Thou, the Lord of glory, should be buffeted and bruised, wounded and killed. This shall not happen unto Thee."

You see that the mistake of the Apostles, and their horror and rejection of what nevertheless was the Eternal and most blessed Truth of the gospel, arose from a religious zeal for the honor of God; though a false zeal. It were well, if the similar mistake of people nowadays had so excellent a source and so good an excuse. For, so it is, that now as then, men are to be found who, with Scripture in their hands, in their memories, and in their mouths, yet make great mistakes as to the meaning of it, and that because they are prejudiced against the true sense of it.

"I speak as to win men" as the Apostle says; "Judge ye what I say." Is it not so, my dear Brethren? Far be it from me to be severe with such, but is it not so, that in this educated and intelligent and great people, there are multitudes, —nay more, the great majority is such, as to have put a false sense on Scripture, and to be violently opposed to the truth on account of this false interpretation?

The Church of Christ walks the earth now, as Christ did in the days of His flesh, and as our Lord fulfilled the Scriptures in what was and what He did then, so the Church fulfils the Scriptures in what she is and what she does now; as Christ was promised, predicted, in the Scriptures as He was then, so is the Church promised, predicted, in the Scriptures in what she is now. Yet the people of this day, though they read the Scriptures and think they understand them, like the Jews then, who read the Scriptures and thought they understood them, do not understand them. Why? Because like the Jews then, they have been taught badly; they have received false traditions, as the Jews had received the traditions of the Pharisees, and are blind when they think they see, and are prejudiced against the truth, and shocked and offended when they are told it.

And, as the Jews then passed over passages in Scripture, which ought to have set them right, so do Christians now pass over passages, which would, if dwelt on, extricate them from their error. For example, the Jews passed over the texts: "They pierced my hands and my feet," "My God, My God, why hast Thou forsaken Me?" "He was rejected of men, a man of sorrows and acquainted with grief,"—which speak of Christ.

And men nowadays pass over such passages as the following which speak of the Church: "Whosesoever sins ye remit, they are remitted to them"; "Thou art Peter and upon this rock I will build my Church"; "Anointing them with oil in the Name of the Lord"; "The Church the pillar and foundation of the truth"; and the like. They are so certain that the doctrine of the one Holy Catholic Church is not true that they will not give their mind to these passages, they pass them over. They cannot tell you what they mean, but they are quite sure they do not mean what Catholics say they mean, because Catholicism is not true. In fact a deep prejudice is on their minds, or what Scripture calls blindness. They cannot tell what these passages and many others mean, but they do not care. They say that after all they are not important—which is just begging the question— and when they are urged and forced to give them a meaning, they say any thing that comes uppermost, merely to satisfy or to perplex the questioner, wishing nothing more than to get rid of what they think a troublesome, but idle, question.

Now is it not strange that persons who act in this way, who skip over things in Scripture, and go by their prejudices, and by the bad teaching they have received in Scripture, should yet boast that they are scriptural and go by Scripture, and use their private judgment? No, they do not judge, they do not examine, they do not go by Scripture; but they take just so much of

Scripture as suits them, and leave the rest. They go, not by their private judgment, but their private prejudice, and by their private liking.

Now I will add one thing more. Persons who act thus are of very different character, just as those who stumbled at our Lord when He came on earth were very different from each other. Both the hard-hearted Pharisees and the tenderhearted Apostles were surprised and shocked at Christ's Passion and death. And so now two sorts of persons are offended at the Holy Church—some are hopeless, other are hopeful. The event shows it. We cannot decide which are the one, which the other, except by the event; but so it is—some are driven further and further from the Church, the more they hear and see of it, and others as time goes on are brought nearer to it, and submit themselves to it.

This being the state of the case, how are we Catholics to behave ourselves to such prejudiced and erring persons? We should imitate our Lord and Master. He was most patient with them; He abounded in long-suffering. "A bruised reed did He not break, and smoking flax did He not quench." He did not argue, but He quietly led them on. He displayed His wonders to them. He gradually influenced them by His words and by His grace, and then enlightened them, till they believed all things.

Till that Apostle, who doubted most stoutly of His Resurrection, cried out, overcome, "My Lord and My God." So must we do now—so does the Church do now. Argument is well in its place, but it is not the chief thing. The chief thing is to win the mind, to melt the heart, to influence the will. This the Church does. After the pattern of her Divine Lord she draws us with cords of a man, with cords of love, with divine charity; "she hopeth all things, endureth all things," she opens the gates of her temple, she lights up her altars, she displays the Most Holy under the sacramental veil, she bursts forth into singing, till the wayward soul, overcome and subdued, says with the Patriarch, "It is enough—let me now die, for I have seen Thy Face; Nunc Dimittis, Lord now lettest Thou Thy servant depart in peace, for mine eyes have seen Thy salvation. I have heard of Thee with the hearing of the ear, but now mine eye seeth Thee." And, as our Lord after His resurrection opened the understanding of the disciples to understand the Scripture, so now are the hearts of men softened and enlightened, and they see that the Church fulfils all the prophecies about herself, all that is written in the Law, the Prophets, and the Psalms; and thus they fall down and worship, and confess that God is here of a truth.

Blessed are they who thus fall down and worship. Blessed are they whom the grace of God leads on to embrace the truth. Blessed who yield their minds to the gentle influences of the Holy Ghost, and stop not till He has brought them on to the haven. But, my Brethren, what I have been saying does not apply exclusively to this or that set of men, but belongs to us all. For all of us, not this or that man only, but all of us, Catholics or not, are led forward by God in a wonderful way— through a way of wonders, a way wonderful to us, a way marvelous, strange, startling, to our natural feelings and tastes, whatever our place in the Church may be. As faith is the fundamental grace, which God gives us, so a trial of faith is the necessary discipline, which He puts upon us. We cannot well have faith without an exercise of faith.

This is implied in the very passage, which has given occasion to the remarks, which I have been making. When the disciples shrank from His words about His own death and passion, what did He do? He met a blind man, and He took him and gave him sight. Why did He give him this special favor? He expressly tells us. He says, "Thy faith hath made thee whole." Here was a tacit rebuke of the slowness to believe in His own disciples and friends, all things are possible to him that believeth. This poor outcast is a lesson to you, O My own people. He puts you to shame. He has had faith in Me, while ye stumble at My word, and when I say a thing, answer "Be it far from Thee, Lord."

The office this day gives us another instance of the same great lesson. The Church reads today the history of the call of Abraham, and meditates upon his great act of obedience, in lifting up his knife to slay his son. Abraham, our father, is our great pattern of faith, and his faith was tried, first by being called on to leave his country and kindred, next by being told to sacrifice his dearly beloved Isaac. The first was trying enough, but what a stumbling block the second might have been to faith less than his. If the disciples were shocked that the divine Antitype should be put to death, surely Abraham too had cause of offence that his own Isaac was to be struck down and slain by him, by his hand, by the hand of his father! Yet he went about the fulfillment of this command, as gravely, as quietly, as calmly, as if it was a mere ordinary action. Thus he showed his faith and gained the blessing.

Be sure, my Brethren, that this must be our way too. Never does God give faith, but He tries it, and none without faith can enter the kingdom of heaven. Therefore all ye who come to serve God, all ye who wish to save your souls, begin with making up your minds that you cannot do so, without a generous faith, a generous self-surrender; without putting yourselves into God's hands, making no bargain with Him, not stipulating conditions, but saying "O Lord here I am—I will be whatever Thou wilt ask me—I will go whithersoever Thou sendest me—I will bear whatever Thou puttest upon me. Not in my own might or my own strength. My strength is very weakness—if I trust in myself more or less, I shall fail—but I trust in Thee—I trust and I know that Thou wilt aid me to do, what Thou callest on me to do—I trust and I know that Thou wilt never leave me nor forsake me. Never wilt Thou bring me into any trial, which Thou wilt not bring me through. Never will there be a failing on Thy part, never will there be a lack of grace. I shall have all and abound. I shall be tried: my reason will be tried, for I shall have to believe; my affections will be tried, for I shall have to obey Thee instead of pleasing myself; my flesh will be tried, for I shall have to bring it into subjection. But Thou art more to me than all other things put together. Thou canst make up to me all Thou takest from me and Thou wilt, for Thou wilt give to me Thyself. Thou wilt guide me."

Reflection.

XII. Surrender to God
First Sunday of Lent, March 12th, 1848

I suppose it has struck many persons as very remarkable, that in the latter times the strictness and severity in religion of former ages has been so much relaxed. There has been a gradual abandonment of painful duties, which were formerly enforced upon all. Time was when all persons, to speak generally, abstained from flesh through the whole of Lent. There have been dispensations on this point again and again, and this very year there is a fresh one. What is the meaning of this? What are we to gather from it? This is a question worth considering. Various answers may be given, but I shall confine myself to one of them.

I answer that fasting is only one branch of a large and momentous duty, the subdual of ourselves to Christ. We must surrender to Him all we have, all we are. We must keep nothing back. We must present to Him as captive prisoners with whom He may do what He will, our soul and body, our reason, our judgment, our affections, our imagination, our tastes, our appetite. The great thing is to *subdue* ourselves; but as to the particular form in which the great precept of self-conquest and self-surrender is to be expressed, that depends on the person himself, and on the time or place. What is good for one age or person, is not good for another.

There are other instances of the same variation. For example, devotion to the Saints is a Catholic practice. It is founded on a clear Catholic doctrine, and the Catholic practice has been the same from the beginning. It could not possibly change. Yet it is certain that the prominent object of that devotion has varied at different times, varying now in the case of individuals, one person having a devotion to one saint, another to another; and in like manner it has varied in the Church at large—for example, quite at first the Martyrs, as was natural, took up this principal attention. It was natural, when their friends were dying daily under the sword or at the stake before their eyes, to direct their devotion in the first instance to their glorified spirits. But when a time of external peace was granted, then the thought of the Blessed Virgin took up its abode in the hearts of the faithful, and there was a greater devotion than before to her. And this thought of the Blessed Virgin has grown stronger and clearer and more influential in the minds of the Church. The devout servants of Mary were comparatively few in the first ages, now they are many.

Again, to take another instance, the present war with evil spirits would seem to be very different from what it was in former ages. They attack a civilized age in a more subtle way than they attack a rude age. We read in lives of saints and others of the evil spirit showing himself and fighting with them face to face, but now those subtle and experienced spirits find it is more to their purpose not to show themselves, or at least not so much. They find it their interest to let the idea of them die away from the minds of men, that being unrecognized, they may do the more mischief. And they assault men in a more subtle way—not grossly, in some broad temptation, which everyone can understand, but in some refined way they address themselves to our pride or self-importance, or love of money, or love of ease, or love of show, or our depraved reason, and thus have really the dominion over persons who seem at first sight to be quite superior to temptation.

Now apply these illustrations to the case in point. From what has been said it follows that you must not suppose that nothing is incumbent on us in the way of mortification, though you have not to fast so strictly as formerly. It is reasonable to think that some other duty of the same general kind, may take its place; and therefore the permission granted us in eating may be a suggestion to us to be more severe with ourselves on the other hand in certain other respects.

And this anticipation is confirmed by the history of our Lord's temptation in the wilderness. It *began*, you will observe, with an attempt on the part of the evil one to make Him break His fast improperly. It *began*, but it did not end there. It was but the first of three temptations, and the other two were more addressed to His mind, not His bodily wants. One was to throw Himself down from the pinnacle, the other the offer of all the kingdoms of the world. They were more subtle temptations. Now I have used the word "subtle" already, and it needs some explanation. By a subtle temptation or a subtle sin, I mean one which it is very difficult to find out. Everyone knows what it is to break the Ten Commandments, the first, the second, the third, and so on. When a thing is directly commanded, and the devil tempts us directly to break it, this is *not* a subtle temptation, but a broad and gross temptation. But there are a great many things wrong, which are not so obviously wrong.

They are wrong as leading to what is wrong or the consequence of what is wrong, or they are wrong because they are the very same thing as what is forbidden, but dressed up and looking differently. The human mind is very deceitful; when a thing is forbidden, a man does not like directly to do it, but he goes to work if he can to get at the forbidden end in some way. It is like a man who has to make for some place. First he attempts to go straight to it, but finds the way blocked up; then he goes round about it. At first you would not think he is going in the right direction; he sets off perhaps at a right angle, but he just makes one little bend, then another, till at length he gets to his point. Or still more it is like a sailing vessel at sea with the wind contrary, but tacking first this way, and then that, the mariners contrive at length to get to their destination. This then is a subtle sin, when it at first seems not to be a sin, but comes round to the same point as an open direct sin.

To take some examples. If the devil tempted one to go out into the highway and rob, this would be an open, bold temptation. But if he tempted one to do something unfair in the course of business, which was to one's neighbor's hurt and to one's own advantage, it would be a more subtle temptation. The man would still take what was his neighbor's, but his conscience would not be so much shocked. So equivocation is a more subtle sin than direct lying. In like manner a person who does not intoxicate himself, may eat too much. Gluttony is a more subtle sin than drunkenness, because it does not show so much. And again, sins of the soul are more subtle sins than sins of the body. Infidelity is a more subtle sin than licentiousness.

Even in our Blessed Lord's case the Tempter began by addressing himself to His bodily wants. He had fasted forty days, and afterwards was hungered. So the devil tempted Him to eat. But when He did not consent, then he went on to more subtle temptations. He tempted Him to spiritual pride, and he tempted Him by ambition for power. Many a man would shrink from intemperance, of being proud of his spiritual attainments; that is, he would confess such things were wrong, but he would not see that he was guilty of them.

Next, I observe that a civilized age is more exposed to subtle sins than a rude age. Why? For this simple reason, because it is more fertile in excuses and evasions. It can defend error, and hence can blind the eyes of those who have not very careful consciences. It can make error plausible, it can make vice look like virtue. It dignifies sin by fine names; it calls avarice proper care of one's family, or industry, it calls pride independence, it calls ambition greatness of mind; resentment it calls proper spirit and sense of honor, and so on.

Such is this age, and hence our self-denial must be very different from what was necessary for a rude age. Barbarians lately converted, or warlike multitudes, of fierce spirit and robust power—nothing can tame them better than fasting. But we are very different. Whether from the natural course of centuries or from our mode of living, from the largeness of our towns or other causes, so it is that our powers are weak and we cannot bear what our ancestors did.

Then again what numbers there are who anyhow must have dispensation, whether because their labor is so hard, or because they never have enough, and cannot be called on to stint themselves in Lent. These are reasons for the rule of fasting not being so strict as once it was. And let me now say, that the rule which the Church now gives us, though indulgent, yet is strict too. It tries a man. One meal a day is trial to most people, even though on some days meat is allowed. It is sufficient, with our weak frames, to be a mortification of sensuality. It serves that end for which all fasting was instituted. On the other hand its being so light as it is, so much lighter than it was in former times, is a suggestion to us that there are other sins and weaknesses to mortify in us besides gluttony and drunkenness. It is a suggestion to us, while we strive to be pure and undefiled in our bodies, to be on our guard lest we are unclean and sinful in our intellects, in our affections, in our wills.

When the old rude age of the world was just ended, and an age which is called light and civilization had begun—I mean in the 16th century—the Providence of Almighty God raised up two saints. One came from Florence, and the other came from Spain, and they met together in Rome. They were as unlike each other as any two men could be, unlike in their history, in their character, in the religious institutes, which ultimately, by God's all-directing grace they were prospered in founding. The Spaniard had been a soldier—his history was exciting. He had been tossed about the world, and, after his conversion he founded a company of spiritual knights or cavaliers, as they may be called, who were bound to a sort of military service to the Holy See. The Florentine had been a saint from a boy, perhaps he never committed a mortal sin, and he was a stationary, home saint. For sixty years he lived in Rome and never left it. St. Philip Neri is the Florentine, and St. Ignatius is the Spaniard.

These two saints, so different from each other, were both great masters in their own persons of the grace of abstinence and fasting. Their own personal asceticism was wonderful, and yet these two great lights, though so different from each other, and so mortified themselves, agreed in this—not to impose bodily afflictions to any great extent on their disciples, but mortification of the spirit, of the will, of the affections, of the tastes, of the judgment, of the reason. They were divinely enlightened to see that the coming age, at the beginning of which they stood, required more than anything else, not mortification of the body (though it needed that too, of course,) but more than it mortification of the reason and the will.

Now then I have got at length, my Brethren, to my practical conclusion. What all of us want more than anything else, what this age wants, is that its intellect and its will should be under a law. At present it is lawless, its will is its own law, its own reason is the standard of all truth. It does not bow to authority, it does not submit to the law of faith. It is wise in its own eyes and it relies on its own resources. And you, as living in the world, are in danger of being seduced by it, and being a partner in its sin, and so coming in at the end for its punishment. Now then let me in conclusion, suggest one or two points in which you may profitably subdue your minds, which require it even more than your bodies.

For example, in respect to curiosity. What a deal of time is lost, to say nothing else, in this day by curiosity, about things, which in no ways concern us. I am not speaking against interest in the news of the day altogether, for the course of the world must ever be interesting to a Christian from its bearing upon the fortunes of the Church, but I speak of vain curiosity, love of scandal, love of idle tales, curious prying into the private history of people, curiosity about trials and offences, and personal matters, nay often what is much worse than this, curiosity into sin. What strange diseased curiosity is sometimes felt about the history of murders, and of the malefactors themselves! Worse still, it is shocking to say, but there is so much evil curiosity to know about deeds of darkness, of which the Apostle says that it is shameful to speak. Many a person, who has no intention of doing the like, from an evil curiosity reads what he ought not to read. This is in one shape or other very much the sin of boys, and they suffer for it. The knowledge of what is evil is the first step in their case to the commission of it. Hence this is the way in which we are called upon, with this Lent we now begin, to mortify ourselves. Let us mortify our curiosity.

Again, the desire of knowledge is in itself praiseworthy, but it may be excessive, it may take us from higher things, it may take up too much of our time—it is a vanity. The Preacher makes the distinction between profitable and unprofitable learning when he says, "The words of the wise are like goads and nails." They excite and stimulate us and are fixed in our memories. "But further than this, my son, inquire not. Of making many books there is no end, and much study" (that is, poring over secular subjects,) "is affliction of the flesh. Let us one and all have an end of the discourse: fear God and keep His Commandments, for this is the whole of man."

Knowledge is very well in its place, but it is like flowers without fruit. We cannot feed on knowledge, we cannot thrive on knowledge. Just as the leaves of the grove are very beautiful but would make a bad meal, so we shall ever be hungry and never be satisfied if we think to take knowledge for our food. Knowledge is no food. Religion is our only food. Here then is another mortification. Mortify your desire of knowledge. Do not go into excess in seeking after truths which are not religious. Again, mortify your reason. In order to try you, God puts before you things which are difficult to believe. St. Thomas's faith was tried; so is yours. He said "My Lord and My God." You say so too. Bring your proud intellect into subjection. Believe what you cannot see, what you cannot understand, what you cannot explain, what you cannot prove, when God says it.

Lastly, bring your will into subjection. We all like our own will—let us consult the will of others. Numbers of persons are obliged to do this. Servants are obliged to do the will of their masters, workmen of their employers, children of their parents, husbands of their wives. Well, in these cases let your will go with that of those who have a right to command you. Don't rebel against it. Sanctify what is after all a necessary act. Make it in a certain sense your own, sanctify it, and get merit from it. And again when you are your own master, be on your guard against going too much by your own opinion. Take some wise counselor or director, and obey him. There are persons who cry out against such obedience, and call it a number of bad names. They are the very persons who need it. It would do them much good. They say that men are made mere machines, and lose the dignity of human nature by going by the word of another. And I should like to know what they become by going by their own will. I appeal to any candid person and ask whether he would not confess that on the whole the world would be much happier, that individuals would be much happier, if they had not a will of their own. For one person who has been hurt by following the direction of another, a hundred persons have been ruined by going by their own will. This is another subject. But this is enough. May almighty God enable you, etc.

Reflection.

XIII. The World and Sin
Second Sunday in Lent, March 19, 1848

In the passage of St. Matthew's Gospel, part of which is read as the Gospel for this day, we have a very remarkable contrast, the contrast between this world and the unseen world. It is so distinctly drawn out, and so impressive, that it may be profitable to us, with God's grace, to attempt to enlarge upon it.

Our Lord often passed the night in prayer, and, as afterwards in that sad night before His passion He took with Him three apostles to witness His prayer in agony, so at an earlier time, He took the same favored three with Him to witness His prayer in ecstasy and glory. On the one occasion He fell on His face and prayed more earnestly till He was covered with a sweat of blood which rolled down upon the cold earth. In the other, as He prayed his countenance became bright and glorious, and He was lifted off the earth. So He remained communing with His Father, ministered to by Moses and Elias, till a voice came from the cloud, which said, "This is My beloved Son, hear ye Him." The sight had been so wonderful, so transporting, that St. Peter could not help crying out. He knew not what he said. He did not know how to express his inward feelings, nor did he understand in a moment all the wonders about him. He could but say, "Lord it is good for us to be here." Simple words, but how much they contain in them. It was good, it was the good of man, it was the great good, it was our good. He did not say that the sight was sublime and marvelous. He was not able to reflect upon it and describe it. His reason did not speak, but his affections. He did but say that it was good to be there. And he wished that great good to continue to him ever. He said "Let us build three tabernacles, one for Thee, one for Moses, and one for Elias." He wished to remain there for ever, it was so good. He was loath the vision should come to an end. He did not like to descend from the mount, and return to those whom he had left behind.

Now let us see what was taking place below, while they were above. When they reached the crowd, they found a dispute going on between the rest of the apostles and the Scribes. The subject of it seems to have been the poor demoniac, who is next spoken of. A father had brought his son to be cured by the apostles. He was a frightful maniac, possessed by the devil. None could hold him. The spirit took away his voice and hearing. He was ordinarily deaf and dumb, but sometimes he dashed himself to the ground, threw himself into the fire or into the water, foamed at the mouth, and then perhaps collapsed. The devil was too much for the apostles. They could not master him, they could not cast him out. They were reduced to a sort of despair, and this was the occasion, as it appears, of their dispute with the Scribes, who might be taunting them with their failure. O the contrast between what St. Peter had come from, and what he had now come to! He had left peace, stillness, contemplation, the vision of heaven, and he had come into pain, grief, confusion, perplexity, disappointment, and debate.

Now this contrast, as I have said, between the Mount of Transfiguration and the scene at its foot, fitly represents to us the contrast between the world and the Church, between the things seen and the things unseen.

I will not dwell on the mere physical evils of this life, though they are enough to appall us, the miseries of sickness, pain, want, cold, hunger; but let us dwell upon the moral evils which it contains. The poor youth who was brought to Christ to be cured, was possessed by the devil, and alas! is not a great portion, is not the greatest portion of mankind at this day possessed by the devil too? He is called in Scripture "the god of this world," and "the Prince of the powers of this air, the spirit which now worketh in the children of disbelief." In the book of Job we read of his "compassing the earth and walking up and down in it," and St. Peter speaks of our "adversary the devil, as a roaring lion, compassing the earth, seeking whom he may devour." Thus he is found all over the earth, and within the souls of men, not indeed able to do anything which God does not permit, but still, God not interfering, he possesses immense power, and is able to influence millions upon millions to their ruin. And as the poor epileptic in the gospel was under the mastery of the evil spirit, so that his eyes, his ears, his tongue, his limbs were not his own, so does that same miserable spirit possess the souls of sinners, ruling them, impelling them here and there, doing what he will with them, not indeed doing the same with every one, some he moves one way, some in another, but all in some pitiable, horrible, and ungodly way.

Wickedness is sometimes called madness in Scripture—so it is. As literal madness is derangement of the reason, so sin is derangement of the heart, of the spirit, of the affection. And as madness was the disorder in which possession by the devil showed itself in Scripture, so this madness of the heart and spirit is the disorder, which in all ages the devil produces in the spirit. And as there are different forms of that madness which is derangement of the reason, so there are different forms of that worse madness which is sin. In an asylum there are different forms of the disorder, and so this whole world is one vast madhouse, of which the inmates, though shrewd enough in matters of this world, yet in spiritual matters are in one way or another mad.

For example, what is the drunkard but a sort of madman? Who is possessed and ruled by an evil spirit, if not he? He has delivered himself over to the power of Satan, and he is his slave. He cannot do what he would. Through his own fault he cannot do what he would. In that he differs from the real madman, whose fault it is not that he is mad; whereas it is the drunkard's own fault that he is the slave of evil. But so it is, he has put himself under the power of evil, he puts himself away from grace, he cannot make up his mind to will to be otherwise, his will is set on what is evil, and thus he is a mere slave. The relentless spirit of evil carries him off to the haunts of intemperance. He knows that he is ruining himself, soul and body, he knows the misery he brings his family, he knows that he is shortening his life, he curses perhaps his own infatuation while he persists in it. He wishes he had never been born. Perhaps he has a bad illness in consequence, and the medical man who attends him, says to him, that it will to a certainty be his death, if he does not reform. He knows it, yet his sin is too strong for him, and in this despair and agony of mind perhaps he takes up some dreadful belief, most injurious to God's honor and glory, as if he were fated to all this, and could not help it. He says, "Every man is fated to be what he is, it can't be helped, it's not my fault, I never could have been otherwise, it did not depend on me." Miserable and most untrue saying. Is it not the saying of a madman? Is it not the word of one possessed with a devil? Here then is one instance in which the demoniac in the gospel may be taken as a type and emblem of the state of the world.

Others are possessed by spirits of a different kind. They are not outrageous, but they are bowed down to the earth, and kept in a close awful captivity. How many, for instance, are there with hard hearts! And what is hardness of heart but a sort of possession by the evil one? The drunkard has often moments of religious feeling, but there are numbers, and they perhaps what the world calls moral, well conditioned men, who seem to have no heart whatever for spiritual subjects. A true Christian cannot hear the name of Christ without emotion, but in this country there are multitudes, poor and rich, who are set upon nothing else whatever but on getting money, and who have no taste whatever for religion. Sometimes, I say, they are poor, and thus they not merely aim to get a livelihood, for this is right, but are engrossed with the thought. Religion seems to them, not a real thing, but a name, and to concern them no more than what is going on in China or Patagonia. It seems beside the mark, and they merely wonder and stare at those who introduce it. The rich again are engrossed with the wish to make their wealth greater, and the pursuit of wealth blocks up the avenues to their hearts, and they have neither time, nor thought, nor love for the great things which concern their peace. What is all this but another possession of the devil, though very different from the former? It is like moping melancholy. The demoniac in the gospel, not only cried out and tore himself, but at other times he became dry or shriveled, which seems to mean a sort of collapse. What is this love of the world, which we see whether in rich or poor, but a sort of shriveling up or collapse of the soul? What then is so like a possession of Satan? And can any state be more fearful than that of an immortal being, who is to live for ever, attempting to live on mortal food, and having no relish for that immortal food, which alone is its true nourishment? 'What is to be your food, my Brethren, when you get into the next world?

Will this mortal food on which you feed now, be present to you then? What are your souls then to feed on? What is to employ them? Nay, what is to possess them? If a soul goes on contentedly, now the slave of the evil one, if he lets the evil one take up a lodgment in his breast, how is he to dislodge him ever? Will not that evil spirit necessarily and inevitably carry down that soul at once to hell, when death comes?
I might go on upon this subject at great length, were it necessary. Accustom yourself to the idea, my Brethren, and a terrible idea it is, that the state of sin is a demoniacal possession. Consider how such a possession of the body is spoken of in Scripture. Consider how the devil tormented the poor suffering body which he was allowed to get hold of. Then consider, what we may so often see now, what a fearful affliction madness is. Then, when you have considered these two things, and got a clear hold of the idea, think that sin is just such a possession of the heart and spirit. It is not that the body is afflicted, as in the case of a demoniac. It is not that the reason is afflicted, as in the case of a madman. But it is that the spirit, the heart, the affections, the conscience, the will, are in the power of an evil spirit, who sways them about at his pleasure. How awful is this!

When then St. Peter, St. James, and St. John came down from the Mount, and saw the miserable youth tormented by an evil spirit, they saw in that youth a figure and emblem of that world of sinners, to whom in due time they were to be sent to preach. But this was not all. They found their brethren disputing with the Scribes, or at least the Scribes questioning with them. Here is another circumstance in which the scene, which they saw resembled the world. The world is full of wrangling and debate, and not unreasonably, because when the heart is wrong, the reason goes wrong too, and when men corrupt themselves and lead bad lives, then they do not see the truth, but have to hunt about after it, and this creates a great confusion.

For instance, suppose a sudden darkness were to fall upon the streets of a crowded city in day time, you may fancy without my telling you what a noise and clamor there would be, foot passengers, carriages, carts, horses all being mixed together. Such is the state of the world. The evil spirit, which worketh in the children of disbelief, the god of this world, as St. Paul says, has blinded the eyes of them that believe not, and hence they are obliged to wrangle and debate, for they have lost their way; and they fall out with each other and one says this and one says that, because they do not see. When men do not *see*, they begin to *reason*. When men do not see, they begin to talk loud. When men do not see, they begin to quarrel. Look around, my Brethren, is it not so? Have not you theories innumerable, arguments interminable offered to you, on all sides? One man says truth is here, another there. Alas, alas, how many religions are there in this great yet unhappy country! Here you have the Scribes wrangling with each other.

There is no end of religions—there are new ones continually. Now if one is true, the other is false; if the new is true, the old are false, if the old are true, the new are false. All cannot be true. Can even a dozen be true, or six, or two? Can more than *one* be true? And which is that one? Thank God, we, my Brethren, know which that one is—that is the true religion, which has been from the beginning and has been always the same. But on all sides there are wranglings and doubtings and disputings, uncertainty and change.

Now I will mention one other respect in which the scene before the three Apostles when they came down from the Mount resembled the world, and that is a still more miserable one. You will observe that their brethren could not cast the evil spirit out. So it is now. There is an immense weight of evil in the world. We Catholics, and especially we Catholic priests, have it in charge to resist, to overcome the evil; but we cannot do what we would, we cannot overcome the giant, we cannot bind the strong man. We do a part of the work, not all.

It is a battle which goes on between good and evil, and though by God's grace we do something, we cannot do more. There is confusion of nations and perplexity. It is God's will that so it should be, to show His power. He alone can heal the soul, He alone can expel the devil. And therefore we must wait for a great deal, till He comes down, till He comes down from His seat on high, His seat in glory, to aid us and deliver us.

In that day we shall enter, if we be worthy, the fullness of that glory, of which the three Apostles had the foretaste in the moment of Transfiguration. All is darkness here, all is bright in heaven. All is disorder here, all is order there. All is noise here, and there is stillness, or if sounds are heard, they are the sweet sounds of the eternal harps on which the praises of God are sung. Here we are in a state of uncertainty: we do not know what is to happen. The Church suffers; her goodly portion, and her choice inheritance suffer; the vineyard is laid waste; there is persecution and war; and Satan rages and afflicts when he cannot destroy.

But all this will be set right in the world to come, and if St. Peter could say at the Transfiguration "It is good to be here," much more shall we have cause to say so when we see the face of God. For then we shall be like our Lord Himself, we shall have glorified bodies, as He had then, and has now. We shall have put off flesh and blood, and receive our bodies at the last day, the same indeed, but incorruptible, spiritual bodies, which will be able to see and enjoy the presence of God in a way which was beyond the three Apostles in the days of their mortality. Then the envious malignant spirit will be cast out, and we shall have nothing to fear, nothing to be perplexed at, for the Lord God shall lighten us, and encompass us, and we shall be in perfect security and peace.

Then we shall look back upon this world, and the trials, and temptations which are past, and what thankfulness, what joy will not rise within us—and we shall look forward; and this one thought will be upon us that this blessedness is to last for ever. Our security has no limit. It is not that we shall be promised a hundred years of peace, or a thousand, but for ever and ever shall we be as we are, for our happiness and our peace will be founded in the infinite blessedness and peace of God, and as He is eternal and happy, so shall we be.

May this be the future portion of you all, my Brethren, and in order to that future bliss may the present blessing of God, the Father, etc.

Reflection.

XIV. Our Lady in the Gospel
Third Sunday in Lent, March 26, 1848

There is a passage in the Gospel of this day, which may have struck many of us as needing some illustration. While our Lord was preaching, a woman in the crowd cried out, "Blessed is the womb that bore Thee and the breasts which Thou hast sucked" (Luke 11). Our Lord assents, but instead of dwelling on the good words of this woman, He goes on to say something further. He speaks of a greater blessedness. "Yea," He says, "but blessed are they who hear the word of God and keep it."

Now these words of our Lord require notice, if it were only for this reason, because there are many persons nowadays who think they are said in depreciation of the glory and blessedness of the Most Holy Virgin Mary; as if our Lord had said, "My Mother is blessed, but my true servants are more blessed than she is." I shall say some words then on this passage, and with a peculiar fitness, because we have just passed the festival of Lady Day, the great feast on which we commemorate the Annunciation, that is, the visit of the Angel Gabriel to her, and the miraculous conception of the Son of God, her Lord and Savior, in her womb.

Now a very few words will be sufficient to show that our Lord's words are no disparagement to the dignity and glory of His Mother, as the first of creatures and the Queen of all Saints. For consider, He says that it is a more blessed thing to keep His commandments than to be His Mother, and do you think that the Most Holy Mother of God did not keep the commandments of God? Of course no one, no Protestant even—no one will deny she did. Well, if so, what our Lord says is that the Blessed Virgin was *more* blessed in that she kept His commandments than because she was His Mother.

And what Catholic denies this? On the contrary we all confess it. All Catholics confess it. The Holy Fathers of the Church tell us again and again that our Lady was more blessed in doing God's will than in being His Mother. She was blessed in two ways. She was blessed in being His Mother; she was blessed in being filled with the spirit of faith and obedience. And the latter blessedness was the greater. I say the Holy Fathers say so expressly. St. Augustine says, "More blessed was Mary in receiving the faith of Christ, than in receiving the flesh of Christ." In like manner St. Elizabeth says to her at the Visitation, "*Beata es quae credidisti*, Blessed art thou who didst believe"; and St. Chrysostom goes so far as to say that she would not have been blessed, even though she had borne Christ in the body, unless she had heard the word of God and kept it.

Now I have used the expression "St. Chrysostom goes *so far* as to say," not that it is not a plain truth. I say, it is a plain truth that the Blessed Virgin would not have been blessed, though she had been the Mother of God, if she had not done His will, but it is an extreme thing to say, for it is supposing a thing impossible, it is supposing that she could be so highly favored and yet not be inhabited and possessed by God's grace, whereas the Angel, when he came, expressly hailed her as full of grace. "*Ave, gratia plena*." The two blessednesses cannot be divided. (Still it is remarkable that she herself had an opportunity of contrasting and dividing them, and that she preferred to keep God's commandments to being His Mother, if she could not have both.) She who was chosen to be the Mother of God was also chosen to be *gratia plena*, full of grace.

This you see is an explanation of those high doctrines which are received among Catholics concerning the purity and sinlessness of the Blessed Virgin. St. Augustine will not listen to the notion that she ever committed sin, and the Holy Council of Trent declares that by special privilege she through all her life avoided all, even venial sin. And at this time you know it is the received belief of Catholics that she was not conceived in original sin, and that her conception was immaculate.

Whence come these doctrines? They come from the great principle contained in our Lord's words on which I am commenting. He says, "More blessed is it to do God's will than to be God's Mother." Do not say that Catholics do not feel this deeply—so deeply do they feel it that they are ever enlarging on her virginity, purity, immaculateness, faith, humility and obedience. Never say then that Catholics forget this passage of Scripture. Whenever they keep the Feast of the Immaculate Conception, the Purity, or the like, recollect it is because they make so much of the blessedness of sanctity. The woman in the crowd cried out, "Blessed is the womb and the breasts of Mary." She spoke in faith; she did not mean to exclude her higher blessedness, but her words only went a certain way. Therefore our Lord completed them. And therefore His Church after Him, dwelling on the great and sacred mystery of His Incarnation, has ever felt that she, who so immediately ministered to it, must have been most holy.

And therefore for the honor of the Son she has ever extolled the glory of the Mother. As we give Him of our best, ascribe to Him what is best, as on earth we make our churches costly and beautiful; as when He was taken down from the cross, His pious servants wrapped Him in fine linen, and laid Him in a tomb in which never man was laid; as His dwelling place in heaven is pure and stainless—so much more ought to be—so much more was—that tabernacle from which He took flesh, in which He lay, holy and immaculate and divine. As a body was prepared for Him, so was the place of that body prepared also. Before the Blessed Mary could be Mother of God, and in order to her being Mother, she was set apart, sanctified, filled with grace, and made meet for the presence of the Eternal.

And the Holy Fathers have ever gathered the exact obedience and the sinlessness of the Blessed Virgin from the very narrative of the Annunciation, when she became the Mother of God. For when the Angel appeared to her and declared to her the will of God, they say that she displayed especially four graces, humility, faith, obedience and purity. Nay, these graces were as it were, preparatory conditions to her being made the minister of so high a dispensation. So that if she had not had faith, and humility, and purity, and obedience, she would not have merited to be God's Mother. Thus it is common to say that she conceived Christ in mind before she conceived Him in body, meaning that the blessedness of faith and obedience preceded the blessedness of being a Virgin Mother. Nay, they even say that God waited for her consent before He came into her and took flesh of her. Just as He did no mighty works in one place because they had not faith, so this great miracle, by which He became the Son of a creature, was suspended till she was tried and found meet for it—till she obeyed.

But there is something more to be added to this. I said just now that the two blessednesses could not be divided, that they went together. "Blessed is the womb," etc.; "Yea, rather blessed," etc. It is true, but observe this. The Holy Fathers always teach that in the Annunciation, when the Angel appeared to our Lady, she showed that she preferred what our Lord called the greater of the two blessednesses to the other. For when the Angel announced to her that she was destined to have that blessedness which Jewish women had age after age looked out for, to be the Mother of the expected Christ, she did not seize the news, as another would, but she waited. She waited till she could be told it was consistent with her Virgin state. She was unwilling to accept this most wonderful honor, unwilling till she could be satisfied on this point. "How shall this be, since I know not man?" They consider that she had made a vow of virginity, and considered that holy estate a greater thing than to bear the Christ. Such is the teaching of the Church, showing distinctly how closely she observes the doctrine of the words of Scripture on which I am commenting, how intimately she considers that the Blessed Mary felt them, viz. that though blessed was the womb that bore Christ and the breasts which He sucked, yet more blessed was the soul which owned that womb and those breasts, more blessed was the soul full of grace, which because it was so gracious was rewarded with the extraordinary privilege to be made the Mother of God.

But now a further question arises, which it may be worth considering. It may be asked, why did our blessed Lord even *seem* to extenuate the honor and privilege of His Mother? When the woman said, "Blessed is the womb," etc., He answered indeed, "*Yea*." But He went on, "Yea, rather blessed." And on another occasion, if not on this, He said when someone told Him that His Mother and brethren were without, "Who is My Mother?" etc. And at an earlier time, when He began His miracles, and His Mother told Him that the guests in the marriage feast had no wine, He said, "Woman, what have I to do with thee? Mine hour is not yet come." These passages seem to be coldly worded towards the Blessed Virgin, even though the sense may be satisfactorily explained. What then do they mean? Why did He so speak?

Now I shall give two reasons in explanation:
1. The first which more immediately rises out of what I have been saying is this: that for many centuries the Jewish women had looked out each of them to be the Mother of the expected Christ, and had not associated it apparently with any higher sanctity. Therefore they had been so desirous of marriage; therefore marriage was held in such special honor by them.

Now marriage is an ordinance of God, and Christ has made it a sacrament—yet there is a higher state, and that the Jews did not understand. Their whole idea was to associate religion with pleasures of this world. They did not know, commonly speaking, what it was to give up this world for the next. They did not understand that poverty was better than riches, ill name than good name, fast and abstinence than feasting, and virginity than marriage. And therefore when the woman in the crowd cried out upon the blessedness of the womb that bore Him and the breasts that He had sucked, He taught her and all who heard Him that the soul was greater than the body, and that to be united to Him in spirit was more than to be united to Him in flesh.

2. This is one reason, and the other is more interesting to us. You know that our Savior for the first thirty years of His earthly life lived under the same roof as His Mother. When He returned from Jerusalem at the age of twelve with her and St. Joseph, it is expressly said that He was subject to them. This is a very strong expression, but that subjection, that familiar family life, was not to last to the end. Even on the occasion upon which the Evangelist says that He was subject to them, He had said and done what emphatically conveyed to them that He had other duties. For He had left them and stayed in the Temple among the doctors, and when they expressed surprise, He answered, "Wist ye not that I ought to be in the things which are My Father's?" This was, I say, an anticipation of the time of His Ministry, when He was to leave His home. For thirty years He remained there, but, as He was steadily observant of His home duties, while they were His duties, so was He zealous about His Father's work, when the time came for His performing it. When the time of His mission came, He left His home and His Mother and, dear as she was to Him, He put her aside.

In the Old Testament the Levites are praised because they knew not father or mother, when duty to God came in the way. "Who said to his father and to his mother, I know you not, and to his brothers, I am ignorant of you" (Deut. 33). "They knew not their children." If such was the conduct of the sacerdotal tribe under the Law, well did it become the great and one Priest of the New Covenant to give a pattern of that virtue which was found and rewarded in Levi. He too Himself has said, "He who loveth father or mother more than Me, is not worthy of Me." And He tells us that "every one who hath left home or brothers or sisters or father or mother or wife or children or lands for His name's sake, shall receive a hundredfold and shall possess eternal life" (Matt. 19). It became then Him who gave the precept to set the example, and as He told his followers to leave all they had for the Kingdom's sake, *in His own Person* to do all that He could, to leave all He had, to leave His home and His Mother, when He had to preach the Gospel.

Therefore, it was that from the beginning of His ministry, He gave up His Mother. At the time He did His first miracle, He proclaimed it. He did that miracle at her bidding, but He implied, or rather declared, that He was then beginning to separate from her. He said, "What is between Me and thee?" And again, "My hour is not yet come," that is, The hour cometh when I shall acknowledge thee again, 0 my Mother. The hour cometh when thou rightly and powerfully wilt intercede with Me. The hour cometh when at thy bidding I will do miracles: it cometh, but it is not yet come. And till it is come "What is between thee and Me? I know thee not. For the time I have forgotten thee."

From that time we have no record of His seeing His Mother till He saw her under His Cross. He parted with her. Once she tried to see Him. A report went about that He was beside Himself. His friends went out to get possession of Him. The Blessed Virgin apparently did not like to be left behind. She went out too. A message came to Him that they were seeking Him, could not reach Him for the press. Then He said those serious words, "Who is My Mother?" etc., meaning, as it would appear, that He had left all for God's service, and that, as for our sake He had been born of the Virgin, so for our sake He gave up His Virgin Mother, that He might glorify His heavenly Father and do His work.

Such was His separation from the Blessed Mary, but when on the Cross He said, "It is finished," this time of separation was at an end. And therefore before it His blessed Mother had joined Him, and He seeing her, recognized her again. His hour was come, and He said to her of St. John, "Woman, behold thy son," and to St. John, "Behold thy Mother."

And now, my Brethren, in conclusion I will but say one thing. I do not wish your words to outrun your real feeling. I do not wish you to take up books containing the praises of the Ever Blessed Virgin, and to use them and imitate them rashly without consideration. But be sure of this, that if you cannot enter into the warmth of foreign books of devotion, it is a deficiency in you. To use strong words will not mend the matter; it is a fault within which can only gradually be overcome, but it is a deficiency, for this reason, if for no other. Depend upon it, the way to enter into the sufferings of the Son, is to enter into the sufferings of the Mother. Place yourselves at the foot of the Cross, see Mary standing there, looking up and pierced with the sword. Imagine her feelings, make them your own. Let her be your great pattern. Feel what she felt and you will worthily mourn over the death and passion of your and her Savior. Have her simple faith, and you will believe well. Pray to be filled with the grace given to her. Alas, you must have many feelings she had not, the feeling of personal sin, of personal sorrow, of contrition, and self hate, but these will in a sinner naturally accompany the faith, the humility, the simplicity which were her great ornaments. Lament with her, believe with her, and at length you will experience her blessedness of which the text speaks. None indeed can have her special prerogative, and be the Mother of the Highest, but you will have a share in that blessedness of hers which is greater, the blessedness of doing God's will and keeping His Commandments.

Reflection.

XV. Stewards and also Sons of God
Eighth Sunday after Pentecost, July 31, 1870

The parable of the unjust steward which is the subject of today's Gospel is more difficult to understand than most of our Lord's Parables—but there are some points in its teaching which it is impossible to mistake.

First, in its literal sense it presents us with a view of human society, as it is, which is true in all ages, now as much as when our Lord spoke. Nothing is more common now in the world than that sort of dishonesty which is instanced in the Unjust Steward. He was in trust with his master's property; he treated it as if it were his own; he wasted it either by carelessness or by spending it on himself. He forgot his duty to his employer, as men do now, and as men now borrow money without rational expectations of repaying it, and thus involve themselves and are unable to meet the claims made on them. Such was the case of the Steward: he was called upon to make his account good, and he could not do so. Under these circumstances he was led on to commit a second sin in order to conceal the first. He took his master's creditors into his counsel, and formed with them a plan of fraudulent returns with the purpose of making his books right. This, I say, is the first picture presented to us in this Parable, and it impresses on us by an instance St. Paul's warning, "The love of money is the root of all evil."

But a larger sense of the parable, and one on which I shall rather insist is this: the view which it gives us of our duties to God and our conduct under those duties. It is plain that the Master spoken of by our Lord is Almighty God Himself; and by the Steward is meant each of His creatures, His rational creatures, who have goods, or, as is sometimes said, talents committed to them, by Him. He does not give these goods to us, but He lends them to us in order that we return them to Him, when our time is ended, with fruit or interest. Men in trade by means of money make money; and as at the end of a certain time capital is thus increased, so by using God's gifts well during the years of this mortal life, we are able to render in to Him a good account and return His gifts with interest. This is the meaning of the Parable of the Talents.

And so as regards the Parable of the Steward, on which I am now remarking, fields and market-gardens and woods yield a produce, and are the means of wealth; such are hay, wheat and other kinds of corn, and various fruits and vegetables in this country; such are olive yards, vineyards, sugar canes, and other produce of the land abroad. As then money creates money, as the land bears bread, wine and oil, so our souls should yield the due return to God for the many gifts, which He has bestowed upon us.

I am speaking of those gifts which belong to our nature, our birth, or our circumstances; gifts of this world. He has given us the means of worshipping Him and doing Him service. He has given us reason, and a certain measure of abilities, more or less. He has given us health, more or less. He has placed us in a certain station of life, high or low. He has given us a certain power of influencing others. He has given us a certain circle of persons, larger or smaller, who depend on us, whom our words and our actions affect for good or for evil, and ought to affect for good. He has given us our share of opportunities of doing good to others. All these are God's gifts to us, and they are given us, not to be wasted, but to be used, to be turned to account. The Steward in the Parable wasted them; and was made responsible for his waste. And so in our own case, we may waste them, as most men waste them; nay worse, we may not only squander them away, we do not know how; but we may actually misapply them, we may use them actually to the injury of Him who has given them to us; but whether we do nothing with them for God, or actually go on to use them to His dishonor and against the interests of truth and religion, (and the latter is more likely than the former, for not to do good with them is in fact to do evil,) anyhow we shall have one day to answer for our use of them.

Thus the parable before us applies to all of us, as having certain goods committed to us by our Divine Master with a day of reckoning for them in prospect.

But this is not all. Charges were brought against the Steward, and his employer called on him to answer them, or rather examined them, and found them well founded. And so it is sometimes with us, that our conscience, which is the voice of God in the soul, upbraids us, brings before us our neglect of duty, the careless, the irreligious, the evil life which we are leading, our disregard of God's commands, glory, and worship; and anticipates that judgment which is to come. Now sometimes this self-accusation leads us to true repentance and change of life—certainly, praise be to God, this is sometimes the case; but more frequently, instead of turning us into the right path, it has the effect of making us go more wrong than we were before. When the Steward found he could not make good what his Lord had a right to demand of him, he had three courses before him besides that which he adopted; he might have made his debts good by extra work; again he might have got friends to have supplied the deficiency; or, he might have thrown himself on his Lord's mercy. He might have digged, or he might have begged; but he rejected both means. "I cannot dig," he said, "to beg I am ashamed." So he went off into a further act of dishonesty to the disadvantage of his master.

And in like manner, we, when we have been unfaithful to our good God and feel compunction for that unfaithfulness, have two modes of recovery: we might dig, that is, we might do works of penance; we might vigorously change our life; we might fight with our bad habits; we might redeem the time; that is, we might dig. But we cannot make up our minds to this laborious course; it is too great a sacrifice; it is above us; we cannot dig. And secondly we might beg; that is, we might pray God to forgive us and to change us; we might go to confess our sin and beg for absolution; we might beg the prayers of others, the prayers of the Saints; but to many men, especially to those who are not Catholics, this is more difficult even than labor: "to beg we are ashamed." Begging seems something inconsistent with what they call the dignity of human nature; they think it unmanly, cowardly, slavish; it wounds their pride to confess themselves miserable sinners, to come to a priest, to say the Rosary, to give themselves to certain devotions, day after day; they think such a course as much beneath them as a valiant effort to overcome themselves is above them. They cannot dig, to beg they are ashamed; and therefore they attempt to destroy the sense of their sins, which has fallen upon them by some means worse than those sins themselves—I mean, such as denying perhaps that there is any such thing as sin, saying that it is a bugbear invented by priests, nay perhaps going so far as to say that there is no judgment to come, no God above who will see and will judge what they say or do.

Such is the repentance of men of the world, when conscience reproaches them. It is not a true turning from sin, but a turning to worse sin—they go on to *deny* the Holy Commandment because they have *transgressed* it; they explain away the sinfulness of sin because they have sinned. St. Paul speaks of this evil repentance, if it may be called by that name, in his Second Epistle to the Corinthians, when he says to them the words of 2 Cor. vii. 10. Such is the state of mankind as we see it realized on a large scale on the face of human society in the world at large. When they do evil, act against their conscience and clear duty, there is this opposition between what they know and what they do; light becomes darkness, and instead of the light within them destroying their tendencies to sin, their sins dim or stifle that light, and they become worse than they were, because they were bad already.
This lesson I draw from today's Gospel.

Now let us turn to today's Epistle, which carries on the lesson farther, and that both for our warning, and for our encouragement and comfort. It is taken from St. Paul's Epistle to the Romans, and begins thus: "Brethren: We are debtors, not to the flesh, to live according to the flesh; for if you live according to the flesh, you shall die." Now here first we must see what is the meaning of the flesh. At first sight it may seem to mean human nature, but that is not its exact meaning. To explain it, I will turn to the 40th chapter of Isaias. In it is the great promise of the coming of Christ, the preaching of His forerunner, St. John Baptist, and the gifts of the Gospel. The Prophet begins, "Be comforted, be comforted, my people," and he speaks of the voice crying in the wilderness ... Then he says, (which is the passage to which I especially refer), "All flesh is grass, and its goodness is like the flower of the field ... " Now is not the grass, and are not the flowers of the field in themselves good? Does not our Lord say that they are more beautiful than Solomon in all his glory? Certainly. But what is their defect? They fade—our Lord says that today they are and tomorrow are cast into the oven. That is the case with the human soul. Of course it cannot die as the flowers of the field; but its first estate dies. Whatever there is of good in it, whatever of virtue, dies out of the soul as life goes on, as the flowers die, as the human body dies; and as the flowers are at length (as our Lord says) cast into the oven, as fuel, fair as they once were, so much more does the moral excellence of man die, as time goes on; and the longer he lives, the harder, the colder, the uglier in God's sight, the deader, I may say, he becomes.

Now we shall see what St. Paul's meaning is. When he speaks of the flesh, he means human nature in its state of decay, in that state into which he is sure to fall, as times goes on; and he says, "If ye live according to the flesh, ye shall die." If, like the Unjust Steward, we live in the mere way of nature, we shall soon lose all the little good that nature has on starting; and become worse and worse, as time goes on, just as the Steward went from one sin to another, till we reach a state of spiritual death. For all flesh is grass; and this is the beginning and end of the matter; this is the end of all our hopes, all our aspirations, as far as nature is concerned—utter, desperate ruin.

And now I come to the light which dawns upon this darkness, the light which rises over against it, illuminating this solemn history; a light by which a lesson which is so painful, so depressing, becomes a consolation and an encouragement. Blessed be God, that though such is the state of nature, God has not left us in a mere state of nature, but has come to our relief, and brought us into a state higher than our own nature, and thereby destroyed this tangle, this web, this bond, in which mankind lies. He has sent to us His dearly beloved Son, Jesus Christ, to give us the gifts of grace, which is a divine power above nature, or what is called supernatural, by which we are able to do what nature of itself cannot do. Isaias says, "All flesh is grass"; but St. Peter in his first Epistle (1 Pet. 1, 24) takes up the word, draws out the happy contrast between nature and grace, and reminds us that by means of the power of grace, what was flesh is flesh no longer, but is spirit; that is, the grace of the Holy Ghost changes our hearts, according to our Lord's words in St. John, "that which is born of the flesh is flesh, but that which is born of the Spirit is spirit."

This great and blessed announcement is made again and again in the New Testament by our Lord and His Apostles; but let me confine myself to what is told us in the Epistle for this day. St. Paul says, "Brethren: we are debtors, not to the flesh, to live according to the flesh." That is, we owe nothing to the flesh. What has the flesh done for us? It is nothing else than the corruption of our nature; the flesh is pride, wrath, hatred, malice, impurity, intemperance, craft, guile; or as St. Paul expressly says himself to the Galatians: "The works of the flesh are manifest, which are ..." (Gal. 5, 19). What then do we owe to the flesh? We owe sin, misery, a bad conscience, displeasure, spiritual death, future punishment. It has done nothing good for us, and cannot—"for if (he continues) you live according to the flesh, you shall die"; and after saying this, he goes on in wonderful words to enlarge on the contrast of our state, if we have, and if we profit by, the gift of the Spirit.

It is by this gift of the Spirit, that is, by the unmerited supernatural grace of God, that we are set free from that law of sin and death, the law of the flesh, which is the state in which we are born. That tangle of the mind by which our best faculties are kept from rising to Almighty God and seeking their true end and doing their duty, and growing in all good, is a bondage, a slavery, and the grace of God sets us free of it, so that we may (as it were) rise on our feet, and become in St. Peter's words good stewards of the manifold gifts of God.

Again this grace not only sets us free, so that instead of being slaves we are able to serve God, but it does something more for us. It would be a great thing, if we were allowed to be faithful servants of God, as the Unjust Steward ought to have been, but grace makes us that and something more; we become not merely servants but even Sons of God. What a second wonderful privilege is this! Though we were slaves of sin and the evil one, He not only sets us free from that slavery, and takes us into His house and His service; but, more than that, He adopts us to be His children. This is a second wonderful gift of grace.

But there is a third: sons are heirs of their Father, and in like manner He gives us an inheritance; and an inheritance as far above any thing which our nature, even though it were ever so perfect, could merit, viz., the sight of Him hereafter, and eternal life. As paradise is beyond any thing, which our sin could inherit, as sin never can merit God's mercy, but simply merits punishment, so human nature, though ever so pure and perfect, could never merit heaven.

These are the great mercies of God which have reversed the state in which we were born, and enabled us to give a good account of our stewardship. He has fortified nature by means of grace; He has overcome the flesh in us by His supernatural aid, and that by three wonderful gifts: first, He has made us faithful servants, whereas without His aid we can be but Unjust Stewards; secondly He makes us not only faithful servants, but dear sons; and thirdly He not only blesses us in this life, but He promises us life everlasting, according to St. Paul's account in today's Epistle, which I will read again ...

What a view this opens on us both of consolation and of solemn thought! Nothing can harm us, the Sons of God, while we remain in our Father's house. Nothing can deprive us of our hope of heaven. But on the other hand how little we understand our privileges; how little we understand the words of the sacred writers about them. May God enlighten our eyes to see what the privileges are—"that you may know what the hope is of His calling, and what are the riches of the glory of His inheritance in the saints" (Eph. 1, 18).

Reflection.

XVI. The Infidelity of the Future
Opening of St. Bernard's Seminary, October 2, 1873

It is no common occasion of thankfulness to the Giver of all good, the Divine Head of the Church, that has led our Right Reverend Father, the Bishop of this Diocese, to call us this morning from our several homes to this place. It is with no common gladness, with no ordinary words of rejoicing and congratulations on their lips, that so many of his priests and of his devout laity have met him here today in consequence of his invitation. At length this seminary is completed and in occupation, which has been for so long a course of years a vision before his mind, and the subject of his prayers and exertions. Years and years ago I have heard him say, that he never could be at rest, till he was enabled by God's mercy to accomplish this great work, and God has heard his persevering prayers and blessed his unwearied exertions. I might say with truth, that even before some of you, my dear Brethren, were born, or at least from the time that you were in your cradles, he, as the chief Pastor of this diocese, when as yet you knew him not, has been engaged in that great undertaking, of which you, by God's inscrutable grace, enjoy the benefits without your own labors.

It is indeed a great event in this diocese, a great event, I may say, in the history of English Catholics, that at length the injunctions of Ecumenical Councils, the tradition of the Church, the desire of the Sovereign Pontiff, are fulfilled among us, and the Bishop's Throne is erected not merely in a dwelling of brick or stone, in the midst of those in whom Christ is to be formed by his teaching, that they in turn may be the edification and light and strength of the generation which is to come after him.

This handing down of the Truth from generation to generation is obviously the direct reason for the institution of seminaries for the education of the clergy. Christianity is one religious idea. Superhuman in its origin, it differs from all other religions. As man differs from quadruped, bird or reptile, so does Christianity differ from the superstitions, heresies, and philosophies which are around it. It has a theology and an ethical system of its own. This is its indestructible idea. How are we to secure and perpetuate in this world that gift from above? How are we to preserve to the Christian people this gift, so special, so divine, so easily hid or lost amid the imposing falsehoods with which the world abounds?

The divine provision is as follows. Each circle of Christians has its own priest, who is the representative of the divine idea to that circle in its theological and ethical aspects. He teaches his people, he catechizes their children, bringing them one and all into that form of doctrine, which is his own. But the Church is made up of *many* such circles. How are we to secure that they may *all* speak one and the same doctrine? and that the doctrine of the Apostles? Thus: by the rule that their respective priests should in their turn all be taught from one and the same centre, viz., their common Father, the Bishop of the diocese. They are educated in one school, that is, in one seminary; under the rule, by the voice and example of him who is the One Pastor of all those collections or circles of Christians, of whom they all in time to come are to be the teachers. Catholic doctrine, Catholic morals, Catholic worship and discipline, the Christian character, life, and conduct, all that is necessary for being a good priest, they learn one and all from this religious school, which is the appointed preparation for the ministerial offices. As youths are prepared for their secular calling by schools and teachers who teach what their calling requires, as there are classical schools, commercial schools, teachers for each profession, teachers of the several arts and sciences, so the sacred ministers of the Church are made true representatives of their Bishop when they are appointed to the charge of the Christian people, because they come from one centre of education and from the tutelage of one head.

Hence it is that St. Ignatius, the Martyr Bishop of Antioch, in the first century of the Church, speaking of the ecclesiastical hierarchy, comparing the union of the sacred orders with the Bishop, likens it to a harp which is in perfect tune. He says in his Epistle to the Ephesians, "It becomes you to concur in the mind of your Bishop, as indeed you do. For your estimable body of clergy, worthy of God, is in exact harmony with your Bishop, as the strings to the harp. Hence it is that in your unanimity and concordant charity Jesus Christ is sung. And one by one you take your parts in the choir, so as to sing with one voice through Jesus Christ to the Father that He may hear your petitions" (ad Eph. 4).

And if at all times this simple unity, this perfect understanding of the members with the Head, is necessary for the healthy action of the Church, especially is it necessary in these perilous times. I know that all times are perilous, and that in every time serious and anxious minds, alive to the honor of God and the needs of man, are apt to consider no times so perilous as their own. At all times the enemy of souls assaults with fury the Church, which is their true Mother, and at least threatens and frightens when he fails in doing mischief. And all times have their special trials, which others have not. And so far I will admit that there were certain specific dangers to Christians at certain other times, which do not exist in this time. Doubtless, but still admitting this, still I think that the trials which lie before us are such as would appall and make dizzy even such courageous hearts as St. Athanasius, St. Gregory I, or St. Gregory VII. And they would confess that dark as the prospect of their own day was to them severally, ours has a darkness different in kind from any that has been before it.
The special peril of the time before us is the spread of that plague of infidelity that the Apostles and our Lord Himself have predicted as the worst calamity of the last times of the Church. And at least a shadow, a typical image of the last times is coming over the world. I do not mean to presume to say that this is the last time, but that it has had the evil prerogative of being like that more terrible season, when it is said that the

elect themselves will be in danger of falling away. This applies to all Christians in the world, but it concerns me at this moment, speaking to you, my dear Brethren, who are being educated for our own priesthood, to see how it is likely to be fulfilled in this country.

And first it is obvious that while the various religious bodies and sects which surround us according to God's permission have done untold harm to the cause of Catholic truth in their opposition to us, they have hitherto been of great service to us in shielding and sheltering us from the assaults of those who believed less than themselves or nothing at all. To take one instance, the approved miracles of the Saints are not more wonderful than the miracles of the Bible. Now the Church of England, the Wesleyans, the Dissenters, nay the Unitarians have defended the miracles of the Bible and thereby have given an indirect protection to the miracles of ecclesiastical history. Nay, some of their divines have maintained certain ecclesiastical miracles, as the appearance of the Cross to Constantine, the subterranean fire in Julian's attempt to build the Jewish Temple, etc. And so again the doctrines of the Holy Trinity, the Incarnation, Atonement, etc., though as strange to the reason as those Catholic doctrines which they reject, have been held by many of these bodies with more or less distinctness, and thereby we have been unassailed when we have taught them. But in these years before us it will be much if those outlying bodies are able to defend their own dogmatic professions. Most of them, nearly all of them, already give signs of the pestilence having appeared among them. And as time goes on, when there will be a crisis and a turning point, with each of them, then it will be found that, instead of their position being in any sense a defense for us, it will be found in possession of the enemy. A remnant indeed may be faithful to their light, as the great Novatian body stood by the Catholics and suffered with them during the Arian troubles, but we shall in vain look for that safeguard from what may be called the orthodoxy of these Protestant communions, which we have hitherto profited by.

Again, another disadvantage to us will arise from our very growth in numbers and influence in this country. The Catholic

Religion, when it has a free course, always must be a power in a country. This is the mere consequence of its divine origin. While Catholics were few and oppressed by disabilities, they were suffered and were at peace. But now that those disabilities are taken off and Catholics are increasing in number, it is impossible that they should not come in collision with the opinions, the prejudices, the objects of a Protestant country, and that without fault on any side, except that the country is Protestant. Neither party will understand the other, and then the old grievances in history which this country has against Rome will be revived and operate to our disadvantage. It is true that this age is far more gentle, kind and generous than former ages, and Englishmen, in their ordinary state, are not cruel, but they may easily be led to believe that their generosity may be abused on our part, that they were unwise in liberating those who are in fact their mortal enemies. And this general feeling of fear of us may be such as, even with a show of reason, to turn against us even generous minds, so that from no fault of ours, but from the natural antagonism of a religion which cannot change with the new political states into which the whole world is gradually molding itself, may place us in temporal difficulties, of which at present we have no anticipation.

And it cannot be denied that there is just now threatening the political world such a calamity. There are many influential men who think that things are not indeed ripe as yet for such a measure, but who look forward to the times, when whether the one or the other great political party in the State may make it their cry at the elections of a new Parliament, that they propose to lessen the influence of Catholics and circumscribe their privileges. And however this may be, two things, I think, are plain, that we shall become more and more objects of distrust to the nation at large, and that our bishops and priests will be associated in the minds of men with the political acts of foreign Catholics, and be regarded as members of one extended party in all countries, the enemies, as will be thought, of civil liberty and of national progress. In this way we may suffer disadvantages, which have not weighed upon the Catholic Church since the age of Constantine.

I repeat, when Catholics are a small body in a country, they cannot easily become a mark for their enemies, but our prospect in this time before us is that we shall be so large that our concerns cannot be hid, and at the same time so unprotected that we cannot but suffer. No large body can be free from scandals from the misconduct of its members. In medieval times the Church had its courts in which it investigated and set right what was wrong, and that without the world knowing much about it. Now the state of things is the very reverse. With a whole population able to read, with cheap newspapers day by day conveying the news of every court, great and small to every home or even cottage, it is plain that we are at the mercy of even one unworthy member or false brother. It is true that the laws of libel are a great protection to us as to others. But the last few years have shown us what harm can be done us by the mere infirmities, not so much as the sins, of one or two weak minds. There is an immense store of curiosity directed upon us in this country, and in great measure an unkind, a malicious curiosity. If there ever was a time when one priest will be a spectacle to men and angels it is in the age now opening upon us.

Nor is this all. This general intelligence of every class of society, general but shallow, is the means of circulating all through the population all the misrepresentations which the enemies of the Church make of her faith and her teaching. Most falsehoods have some truth in them; at least those falsehoods which are perversions of the truth are the most successful. Again, when there is no falsehood, yet you know how strange truth may appear to minds unfamiliar with it. You know that the true religion must be full of mysteries—and therefore to Catholicism, if to any profession, any body of men at all, applies the proverb that a fool may ask a hundred questions which a wise man cannot answer. It is scarcely possible so to answer inquiries or objections on a great number of points of our faith or practice, as to be intelligible or persuasive to them. And hence the popular antipathy to Catholicism seems, and will seem more and more, to be based upon reason, or common sense, so that first the charge will seem to all classes of men true that the Church stifles the reason of man, and next that, since it is impossible for educated men, such as her priests, to believe what is so opposite to reason, they must be hypocrites, professing what in their hearts they reject.

I have more to say on this subject. There are, after all, real difficulties in Revealed Religion. There are questions, in answer to which we can only say, "I do not know." There are arguments which cannot be met satisfactorily, from the nature of the case —because our minds, which can easily enough understand the objections, are not in their present state able to receive the true answer. Nay, human language perhaps has not words to express it in. Or again, perhaps the right answer is possible, and is set down in your books of theology, and you know it. But things look very different in the abstract and the concrete. You come into the world, and fall in with the living objector and inquirer, and your answer you find scattered to the winds. The objection comes to you now with the force of a living expositor of it, recommended by the earnestness and sincerity with which he holds it, with his simple conviction of its strength and accompanied by all the collateral or antecedent probabilities, which he heaps around it. You are not prepared for his objection being part of a system of thought, each part of which bears one way and supports the other parts. And he will appeal to any number of men, friends or others, who agree with him, and they each will appeal to him and all the rest to the effect that the Catholic view and arguments simply cannot be supported. Perhaps the little effect you produce by the arguments which you have been taught is such that you are quite disheartened and despond.

I am speaking of evils, which in their intensity and breadth are peculiar to these times. But I have not yet spoken of the root of all these falsehoods—the root as it ever has been, but hidden; but in this age exposed to view and unblushingly avowed—I mean, that spirit of infidelity itself which I began by referring to as the great evil of our times, though of course when I spoke of the practical force of the objections which we constantly hear and shall hear made to Christianity, I showed it is from this spirit that they gain their plausibility. The elementary proposition of this new philosophy which is now so threatening is this—that in all things we must go by reason, in nothing by faith, that things are known and are to be received so far as they can be proved. Its advocates say, all other knowledge has proof—why should religion be an exception? And the mode of proof is to advance from what we know to what we do not know, from sensible and tangible facts to sound conclusions. The world pursued the way of faith as regards physical nature, and what came of it? Why, that till three hundred years ago they believed, because it was the tradition, that the heavenly bodies were fixed in solid crystalline spheres and moved round the earth in the course of twenty-four hours. Why should not that method which has done so much in physics, avail also as regards that higher knowledge which the world has believed it had gained through revelation? There is no revelation from above. There is no exercise of faith. Seeing and proving is the only ground for believing. They go on to say, that since proof admits of degrees, a demonstration can hardly be had except in mathematics; we never can have simple knowledge; truths are only probably such. So that faith is a mistake in two ways. First, because it usurps the place of reason, and secondly because it implies an absolute assent to doctrines, and is dogmatic, which absolute assent is irrational. Accordingly you will find, certainly in the future, nay more, *even now, even now*, that the writers and thinkers of the day do not even believe there is a God. They do not believe either the *object*—a God personal, a Providence and a moral Governor; and secondly, what they *do* believe, viz., that there is some first cause or other, they do not believe with faith, absolutely, but as a probability.

You will say that their theories have been in the world and are no new thing. No. Individuals have put them forth, but they have not been current and popular ideas. Christianity has never yet had experience of a world simply irreligious. Perhaps China may be an exception. We do not know enough about it to speak, but consider what the Roman and Greek world was when Christianity appeared. It was full of superstition, not of infidelity. There was much unbelief in all as regards their mythology, and in every educated man, as to eternal punishment. But there was no casting off the idea of religion, and of unseen powers who governed the world. When they spoke of Fate, even here they considered that there was a great moral governance of the world carried on by fated laws. Their first principles were the same as ours. Even among the sceptics of Athens, St. Paul could appeal to the Unknown God. Even to the ignorant populace of Lystra he could speak of the living God who did them good from heaven. And so when the northern barbarians came down at a later age, they, amid all their superstitions, were believers in an unseen Providence and in the moral law. But we are now coming to a time when the world does not acknowledge our first principles. Of course I do not deny that, as in the revolted kingdom of Israel, there will be a remnant. The history of Elias is here a great consolation for us, for he was told from heaven that even in that time of idolatrous apostasy, there were seven thousand men who had not bowed their knees to Baal. Much more it may be expected now, when our Lord has come and the Gospel been preached to the whole world, that there will be a remnant who belong to the soul of the Church, though their eyes are not opened to acknowledge her who is their true Mother. But I speak first of the educated world, scientific, literary, political, professional, artistic—and next of the mass of town population, the two great classes on which the fortunes of England are turning: the thinking, speaking and acting England. My Brethren, you are coming into a world, if present appearances do not deceive, such as priests never came into before, that is, so far forth as you do go into it, so far as you go beyond your flocks, and so far as those flocks may be in great danger as under the influence of the prevailing epidemic.

That the discipline of a seminary is just that which is suited to meet the present state of things, it does not become me to attempt to suggest to you now—you, who have so much better, and so much more authoritative advisers—but I may be allowed perhaps to follow up what I have said to such conclusions as it seems to point to.

A seminary is the only true guarantee for the creation of the ecclesiastical spirit. And this is the primary and true weapon for meeting the age, not controversy. Of course every Catholic should have an intelligent appreciation of his religion, as St. Peter says, but still controversy is not the instrument by which the world is to be resisted and overcome. And this we shall see

if we study that Epistle, which comes with an authority of its own, as being put by the Holy Spirit into the mouth of him who was the chief of the Apostles. What he addresses to all Christians, is especially suitable for priests. Indeed he wrote it at a time when the duties of one and the other, as against the heathen world, were the same. In the first place he reminds them of what they really *were* as Christians, and surely we should take these words as belonging especially to us ecclesiastics. "You are a chosen generation, a kingly priesthood, a holy nation, a purchased people ..." (1 Pet. ii. 9). In this ecclesiastical spirit, I will but mention a spirit of seriousness or recollection. We must gain the habit of feeling that we are in God's presence, that He sees what we are doing; and a liking that He does so, a love of knowing it, a delight in the reflection, "Thou, God, seest me." A priest who feels this deeply will never misbehave himself in mixed society. It will keep him from over-familiarity with any of his people; it will keep him from too many words, from imprudent or unwise speaking; it will teach him to rule his thoughts. It will be a principle of detachment between him and even his own people; for he who is accustomed to lean on the Unseen God, will never be able really to attach himself to any of His creatures. And thus an elevation of mind will be created, which is the true weapon which he must use against the infidelity of the world. (Hence, what St. Peter says: 1, ii, 12, 15; iii, 16.)
Now this I consider to be the true weapon by which the infidelity of the world is to be met.

And lastly, most important in the same warfare, and here too you will see how it is connected with a seminary, is a sound, accurate, complete knowledge of Catholic theology. This, though it is not controversial, is the best weapon (after a good life) *in* controversy. Any child, well instructed in the catechism, is, without intending it, a real missioner. And why? Because the world is full of doubtings and uncertainty, and of inconsistent doctrine—a clear consistent idea of revealed truth, on the contrary, cannot be found outside of the Catholic Church. Consistency, completeness, is a persuasive argument for a system being true. Certainly if it be inconsistent, it is not truth.

Reflection.

C. GENERAL REFLECTION ON NEWMAN'S SERMONS.

Printed in Great Britain
by Amazon

57804315R00076